ACTIVATORS

CYCLING

Clive Gifford

Illustrated by Nick Dewar
Consultant: Chris Juden,
CTC Technical Officer

*Hodder
Children's
Books*

a division of Hodder Headline plc

Hodder Children's Books
a division of Hodder Headline plc
338 Euston Road
London NW1 3BH

Meet the author

Clive's coveted yellow jersey was not earned in the Tour de France, but bought from a cycle shop on the Edgware Road in London. This fact, however, has not deterred him from huffing and puffing his way along country lanes and muddy trails over the years. His most exciting trip was down the steep volcanic hills around Lake Rotorua in New Zealand.

His distinct lack of fitness may have prevented him from racing against Chris Boardman and other top riders, but Clive has written about them and their amazing, state-of-the-art bikes for a number of magazines.

All of Clive's cycling friends are fitter and faster than him, but that hasn't stopped them sharing their knowledge and top tips. Clive's a keen cyclist. So keen, in fact, that he celebrated completing this book with a week-long cycle tour around East Anglia.

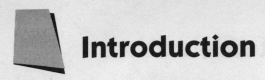

Introduction

Why cycle?

It's a fast, cheap and efficient way of getting from A to B. It's pollution free and ecologically sound, one of the best ways to exercise and most important of all, it's a lot of fun. Don't doubt it: 800 million cyclists agree.

And there's more. These days, all the fashion mags feature cycle-styled gear. Cycling has become the last word in cool.

No I don't own a bike, darling. I just love the clothes.

Cycling gives you good exercise and is much faster, more exciting and less tiring than walking. If energy saving isn't what you're into, then you can arrange competitions, go touring, race on tracks or cycle off-road on trails and tracks where cars simply can't go. Have fun!

Clive

Contents

Types of bike

Mountain bikes

DRAGSTER OR HIGH-RISER

Saddle is perched on a high seat post. This makes it easier for the rider to dismount. ▶

How to mount

Over the years, many bikes have been built. Your parents may have been lumbered with a high-riser – these were thought to be groovy at the time, but were terrible to ride, hard to control and really slow. Luckily, today, you're more likely to own a racer, a tourer, a hybrid, or the current, most popular model, the mountain bike (MTB).

REAR SPROCKETS

REAR GEAR MECHANISM

Tough as nails, mountain bikes are for off-road riding over rough country trails. Most of their fittings are heavy duty, but bike makers have worked hard to try and keep their overall weight down.

You can learn loads more about mountain biking in chapter 6.

15, 18 or 21 gears are common. The gear shifters are usually mounted on the handlebars for easier control.

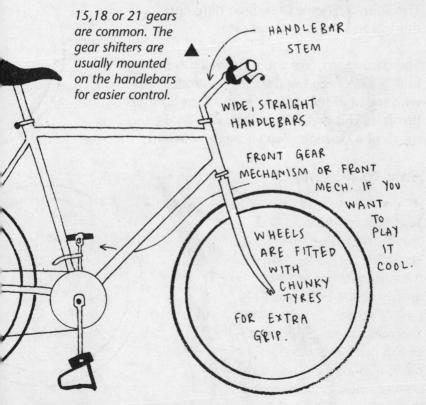

HANDLEBAR STEM

WIDE, STRAIGHT HANDLEBARS

FRONT GEAR MECHANISM OR FRONT MECH. IF YOU WANT TO PLAY IT COOL.

WHEELS ARE FITTED WITH CHUNKY TYRES FOR EXTRA GRIP.

The bottom bracket and chainwheel are set higher from the ground than on regular bikes so that the pedals clear bumps more easily.

7

Racers and touring bikes

You can recognise these by the slim tubing of their frames and their dropped handlebars. Pushed off the number one slot in the cycle charts by the mountain bike, they're now making a comeback.

Narrow tyres grip the road without losing much speed.

There's a bewildering number of specific types of racing bikes – each one designed for a different type of race, tour or competition. The Tour de France uses three different models and that's just one race.

Standard racers, like you may well have, are built for cycling long distances on roads and with speed in mind. They're made as light as possible. This means that they won't take too much of a bashing. **You've been warned!**

This is a standard racer. It's sometimes called a sports bike.

Gear shifters are often found on the down tube. But top racers have shifters built into the brake levers.

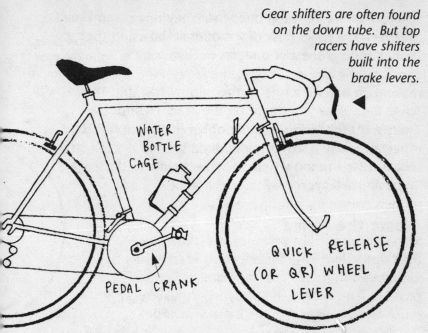

WATER BOTTLE CAGE

PEDAL CRANK

QUICK RELEASE (OR QR) WHEEL LEVER

Touring bikes look similar to racers, but have a stronger frame and medium width tyres so they can carry extra luggage. (You can learn all about this in chapter 7). Their gears and brakes are the same as on a mountain bike.

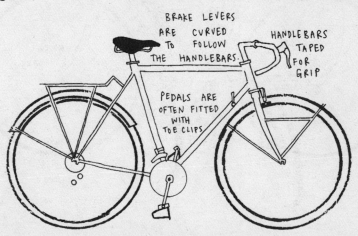

BRAKE LEVERS ARE CURVED TO FOLLOW THE HANDLEBARS.

HANDLEBARS TAPED FOR GRIP

PEDALS ARE OFTEN FITTED WITH TOE CLIPS

9

Hybrid bikes

Hybrids are currently all the rage. They're a compromise between the toughness of a mountain bike and the speed and lightness of a racer.

Mountain bikes are king of the bumpy trail, but their wide tyres slow you down on the road. Hybrids have narrower tyres with some knobbly bits for grip off-road. They also have a larger frame. Hybrid bikes are becoming popular for touring where the rider wants to do some light off-road cycling.

Name the frame

Here's a typical hybrid bike.

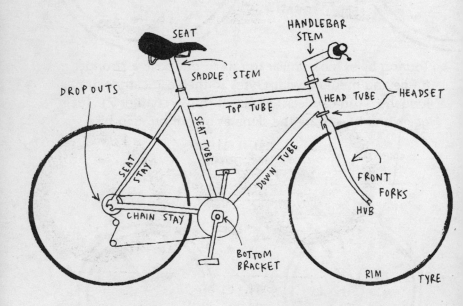

Sizing a frame and wheels

A frame is measured from the top of the seat tube to
the centre of the bottom bracket.

The distance between the centre of each wheel is called
the wheelbase.

Wheel size is given as *width minus rim diameter*. A hybrid
wheel's width is somewhere between the wide 55 mm of a
mountain bike and the narrow 25 mm of a racer/tourer.

*You can learn more
about adjusting bikes for
maximum performance
on pages 16-17.*

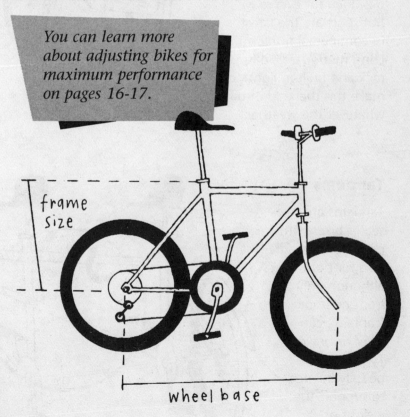

frame
size

wheel base

Other bikes

The bikes already mentioned aren't the only ones around. Here are some more common ones.

City slickers

Many people want a bike without high performance features, just to cycle around town and bikes specially designed for everyday transport are the latest in continental fashion. Long mudguards, a luggage rack and built-in lighting system

ROADSTER.

make this the kind of bike you can just get on and ride whatever the weather.

Tandems

Tandems are two-seater bikes with pedals and handle-bars for both riders although only the front rider, or 'captain', can steer or brake. Tyres have to be fully inflated to support the weight of two riders.

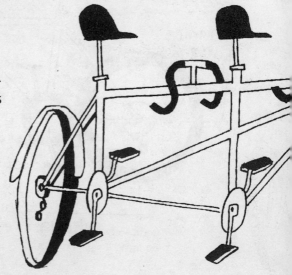

Fold and go

The dream of many cyclists is a bike that folds down to make carrying easier. Advances in materials and design now mean you can get a bike, like the Micro built by Cresswell Cycles, light enough to be carried in one hand.

THE CRESSWELL MICRO PORTABLE BIKE.

Special needs

Being disabled doesn't mean you have to miss out on all that cycling offers. Companies have designed a range of bikes for those with special needs. These include bikes powered by hand-operated pedals, and devices which convert wheelchairs into cycles.

HAND-CYCLE

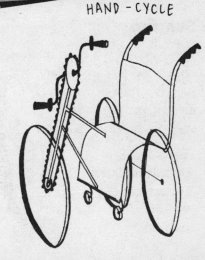

Hand-cycles which attach on to the front of a wheelchair are operated by both arms pushing and pulling and are a great way to keep fit.

Brilliant bikes

Laid-back

Human Powered Vehicles (HPVs) have broken many records on research tracks and are now finding their way on to the streets. The rider is supported in a much more aerodynamic position, which makes a big difference at high speeds.

This Kingcycle Bean HPV managed an incredible 75.6 km in one hour, 20 km/h more than the record for a regular bike.

You may think a tandem or an HPV is strange. They're nothing compared to these mad creations.

Sun fun

The Neufeld is a road bike converted to carry solar panels which power its electric motor. Its top speed is around 35 km/h.

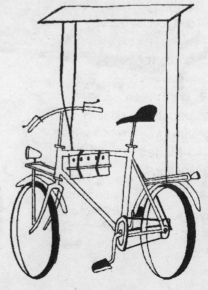

NEUFELD BIKE

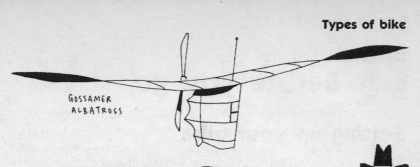

GOSSAMER ALBATROSS

Just PLANE crazy

A plane powered by a bike? Don't laugh. They've been quite successful. The Gossamer Albatross with its 28 m wingspan managed to fly the English Channel. It was purely powered by one very fit cyclist, or should that be pilot, by the name of Bryan Allen.

Fish out of water

The Flying Fish is the world's fastest pedal powered water vehicle. Over a short, 100 m distance it can travel at 30 km/h with its pedals driving a two-bladed propeller.

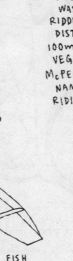

THIS 31m HIGH UNICYCLE WAS ACTUALLY RIDDEN OVER A DISTANCE OF 100m IN LAS VEGAS BY STEVE McPEAK. GOOD NAME FOR HIGH RIDING, HUH?

FLYING FISH

Before you go

Setting up your bike

Your saddle and handlebars are what influence your riding position. You want to be comfy, able to control your bike and maximise your leg power. Saddle and handlebars are easily adjustable with a spanner or Allen key.

Get a friend to hold your bike as you get on it, or use a wall for support. With one pedal at its lowest point, your leg should be nearly but not quite straight. If that's not the case, you will need to adjust the height of the saddle.

This is easy. At the top of the seat tube is a bolt or lever. Undoing this will allow you to raise or lower the saddle.

seat bolt

seat lever

Handlebars

Handlebars should be about level with the saddle. They can be higher for easy riding and maybe a little lower for racing. To change the height, loosen the stem bolt or Allen key fitting and pull the handlebar stem up or push down. You can change the handlebar angle so that you can reach brake and gear controls more easily. You can do this by loosening the stem clamp which holds the handlebars in place.

Seat and handlebar stems have a marked safety line. Don't raise them above this line. Whenever you adjust your saddle or handlebars, make sure that they are straight and tightened afterwards.

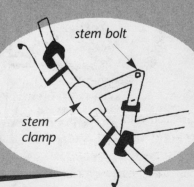

stem bolt

stem clamp

17

All the gear

If you really want to spend a fortune on groovy cycling clothes and accessories, fine. But cycling doesn't have to be a fashion show. You can cycle perfectly well without loads of specialist gear.

The clothes you wear should allow you movement but not be so baggy that they get caught in the bike.

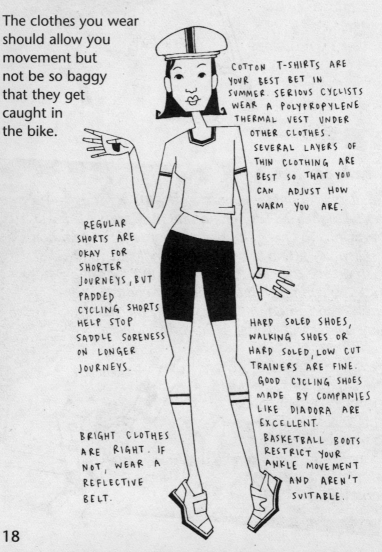

COTTON T-SHIRTS ARE YOUR BEST BET IN SUMMER. SERIOUS CYCLISTS WEAR A POLYPROPYLENE THERMAL VEST UNDER OTHER CLOTHES. SEVERAL LAYERS OF THIN CLOTHING ARE BEST SO THAT YOU CAN ADJUST HOW WARM YOU ARE.

REGULAR SHORTS ARE OKAY FOR SHORTER JOURNEYS, BUT PADDED CYCLING SHORTS HELP STOP SADDLE SORENESS ON LONGER JOURNEYS.

HARD SOLED SHOES, WALKING SHOES OR HARD SOLED, LOW CUT TRAINERS ARE FINE. GOOD CYCLING SHOES MADE BY COMPANIES LIKE DIADORA ARE EXCELLENT. BASKETBALL BOOTS RESTRICT YOUR ANKLE MOVEMENT AND AREN'T SUITABLE.

BRIGHT CLOTHES ARE RIGHT. IF NOT, WEAR A REFLECTIVE BELT.

Essential headwear

Helmets save lives. Top riders wear them, so what's your problem? In Australia, riding without one is against the law. Always buy a quality helmet recommended by a good bike shop. Make sure it fits well, low over your forehead, chin strap tight but comfortable.

WHEN ADJUSTING HELMET STRAPS, MAKE SURE YOU ADJUST BOTH SIDES EQUALLY.

Glove compartment

Cycle mitts protect your hands from blisters and grazes if you fall off. The open fingered gloves give you most control. Some even have gel inside them so the palms of your hands absorb the shock of bumps, and they may have a towelling wipe sewn into the back.

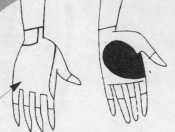

Towelling area on glove.

19

The five minute check

Gremlins exist. Fact. Somehow, these creatures can turn yesterday's perfectly-working bike into today's deathtrap. Do a five minute set of checks before you hop on.

1 Turn the pedals. Does the chain squeak? If it does, it will need lubricating (see page 58).

2 Check that there are no thorns or sharp stones digging into your tyres. Also check the tyre pressures (see page 24).

4 Gently spin the front and back wheels. Do the brake blocks rub against the wheel at any point? If they do, check that the wheel runs true (see page 65) and adjust the brakes.

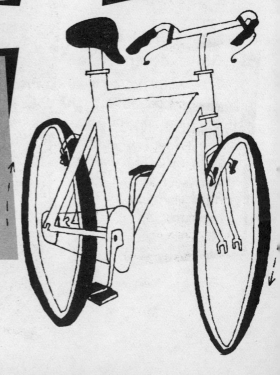

Check the handlebars are aligned so that they form a perfect cross shape with the front wheel. Check the handle-bar stem is tight by standing with the front wheel locked firmly between your legs. Twist the handlebars. If the stem moves, it needs tightening.

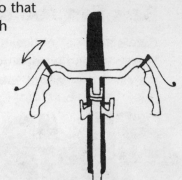

3 Check that all nuts, screws and fittings are nice and tight.

5 Make sure the saddle is in the correct position for you. Check that it won't tilt back or forth or slip down into the seat tube under pressure.

Brakes

Gremlins specialise in brakes and brakes are the most important part of your bike. Give them the full checking treatment, particularly the brake blocks.

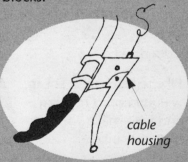

cable housing

Check that the brake levers are not stiff when pulled. If they are, spray some lubricant inside the cable housings.

21

Be smart, be seen

Cycles aren't as noticeable as other, bigger motor vehicles.
Stealth cycling is not a good thing. You risk a major accident
if a car driver cannot spot you easily.

*Bright clothing is a must.
Most cycle gear comes in
a range of lurid fluorescent
colours. Fashion-wise, if
you're more into black
or dark blue, fine, just
so long as you wear a
reflective belt.*

Customise your favourite cycling T-shirt by sewing or
ironing on reflective tape. It looks good, costs little
and really helps you to be seen.

Bike reflectors are cheap,
weigh next to nothing
and help make you
that little bit
more visible.
Here are some
places you
can put them:

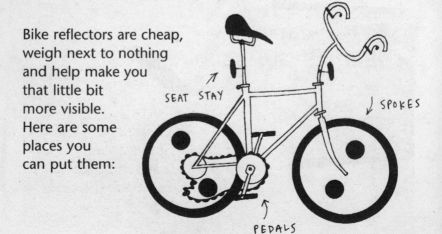

SEAT STAY

SPOKES

PEDALS

Lights

At night, in fog and in poor light conditions, make sure you have decent cycle lights. Dynamo lights get their power from the bike wheels spinning.
They cost nothing to run and are environmentally sound – but the trouble is, apart from expensive models, when the wheels are spinning slowly they dim, and when you stop, they stop.

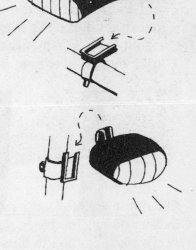

For riding in traffic especially, it is better to use battery-powered lights. Get lights which just pull out of their clip so that when leaving your bike you can take them with you. The front white light also makes a handy torch for map reading.

For long cycles in the dark, carry spare sets of batteries.

Before you go check-list

1: full water bottle
2: some money or a card for the phone – always useful if your bike breaks down
3: minimum repair kit (see page 56)
4: bike lock if stopping at any time (see page 26)
5: helmet
6: bright clothes
7: lights and spare batteries

Pump it up!

Pumping up a cycle's tyres can be a drag, but it's far worse huffing along a road with incorrectly-inflated tyres losing you speed or control.

Under-inflated tyres slow you down enormously. Just as bad, they wear out more quickly and suffer more punctures. But don't over-inflate your tyres or they might burst. In either case, you'll face a bill for new tyres much earlier than if they were inflated correctly.

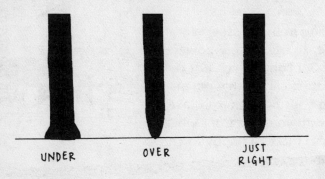

UNDER   OVER   JUST
                            RIGHT

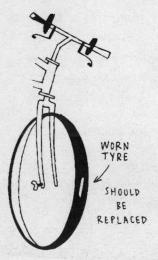

WORN
TYRE

SHOULD
BE
REPLACED

Tired tyres

You should regularly check tyre wear. Any gaps in the rubber grooves or knobbles, known as the tyre's tread, can mean problems.

The cost of inflation

Need a bike pump? Plenty of expensive, groovy, quarter-size and compressed gas models on the market. Forget 'em. An ordinary pump and a tyre pressure gauge will do the business. Check out which type of tyre valve you have before buying though.

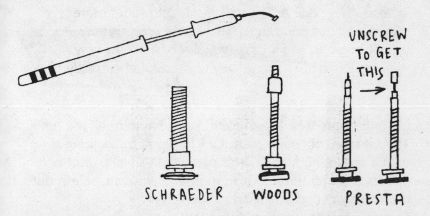

UNSCREW TO GET THIS →

SCHRAEDER   WOODS   PRESTA

PSI OK?

Tyre pressure is measured in pounds per square inch shortened to psi. What is the correct tyre pressure? An approximate guide is written on the side, or wall, of your bike tyre. Go to the top end of the range to provide a harder, faster ride on smooth roads. Reduce it a little below the figure to give a more comfortable ride over slightly rough ground.

Use your pressure gauge to check you have the right pressure and make sure the valve cap is always replaced after pumping.

Spotlight on security

QUIZ
How many bikes are stolen each year in Britain?

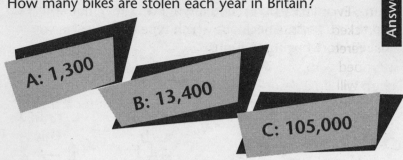

A: 1,300

B: 13,400

C: 105,000

Answer is C

No one wants their bike nicked, yet it happens all the time. The solution, of course, is to lock it. Don't muck around with a cheap, light chain and padlock. A small pair of bolt cutters will snip through it in moments. Instead, splash out on a heavy D-Lock made from solid steel.
They are quite expensive, but a lot cheaper than a new bike.

Loose parts

A D-lock secures your bike frame, but it won't save some of the more easily removable parts. Take these off and keep them with you if you're leaving your bike for a while.

I only need six seconds.

Risky business

Never leave your bike unlocked. It takes an expert thief just seconds to whisk a bike away. Try to lock it in a public place. Even locked, there is sadly still a chance that it will be nicked. But there is some good news; many bikes are recovered. To let the police know whose bike it is, get yours stamped with your house number and postcode. A bike shop will do it. Your bike may be covered on your parents' house insurance, or you may be able to add it for a small extra sum. It's worth checking to see.

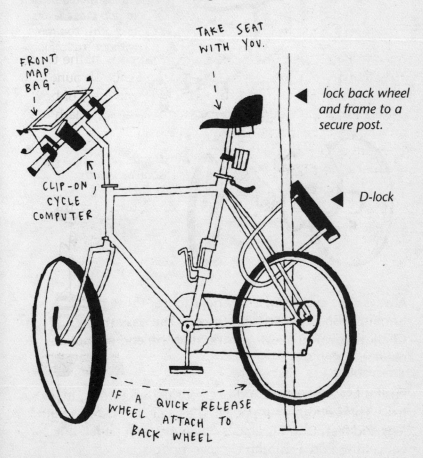

FRONT MAP BAG

TAKE SEAT WITH YOU.

lock back wheel and frame to a secure post.

CLIP-ON CYCLE COMPUTER

D-lock

IF A QUICK RELEASE WHEEL ATTACH TO BACK WHEEL

3 Cool control

Some basics

Let's look at the basic riding position from a different angle.

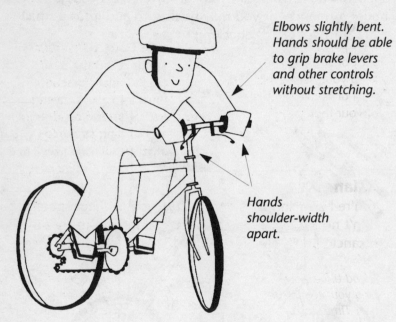

Elbows slightly bent. Hands should be able to grip brake levers and other controls without stretching.

Hands shoulder-width apart.

Always start cycling in a low gear to get those pedals turning at speed right from the off. The easiest way? Change down to a low gear right at the end of your previous ride.

Push off with one foot and get your pedals turning in a low gear. Think about your pedalling as a circle made by your legs and feet. Don't just stab down on each pedal, but concentrate on a smooth circular motion.

START OF STROKE

Foot pushes down from start of stroke. Always keep your heel level with or above the ball of your foot.

BOTTOM OF STROKE

This is called the dead point. Pedalling action turns into a kick, taking pedal past the dead point and starting stroke for other pedal.

Balance

You're balancing all the time you cycle. At high speeds you don't notice, but here's a little game for you to try out your balancing skills at low speed.

Friend times how long you stay in the box. Time starts when front wheel crosses this line.

Time stops when a foot is put down or when bike wheel crosses any other line. Peg down some brightly coloured string on grass. Mark box out on concrete with chalk.

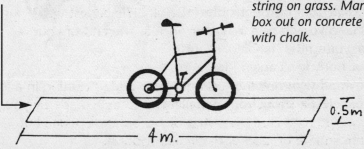

0.5m

4 m.

Steering

Round the bend

Slow down as you come to
a corner or turn. At most
corners you can just
stop pedalling before
and freewheel
round. But if you're
travelling at a high
speed or the
corner is sharp,
use your brakes
to slow down
BEFORE you
reach the turn.
Look to have
changed down the
gears before you
reach the corner, too.
As you approach the
turn leave your inside
pedal up to avoid catch-
ing the ground. Use your
hips to lean into the turn.
Follow your bike's lean with
a gentle turn of the handlebars. As you come out of the
turn, bring the handlebars and
your body level again. Being in
a low gear gives you the chance
to accelerate away from the corner.

Super slalom

Turn turning into a game. Set out a slalom course of stones (mainly between 2 and 4 m apart) on a stretch of grass. Make the turns different sizes and angles.

There's more on close control games on pages 40–41.

Quick steer

This is an advanced way to steer round an obstacle without losing much speed. It's worth trying out with a cardboard box or a chalk line as your first obstacle.

Cut your speed a small amount and turn your handlebars towards the obstacle. What? That's what I said. You see, doing this makes your bike lean away from the obstacle. As your bike leans, steer away from the obstacle. This move allows you to make a sharp turn without losing balance or control.

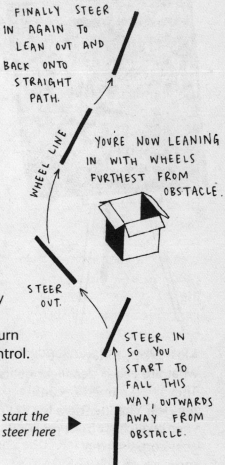

FINALLY STEER IN AGAIN To LEAN OUT AND BACK ONTO STRAIGHT PATH.

WHEEL LINE

YOU'RE NOW LEANING IN WITH WHEELS FURTHEST FROM OBSTACLE.

STEER OUT.

STEER IN SO YOU START TO FALL THIS WAY, OUTWARDS AWAY FROM OBSTACLE.

start the steer here ▶

31

Gears 1

What are gears for?

The answer is, er, all three, but C is by far the most important.

A: To give show-offs a chance to boast how many their bike has.
B: To allow tech-heads the chance to fiddle and maintain them forever.
C: To massively improve your cycling performance.

Gears make cycling a lot easier. They allow you to both travel at high speeds on the level and to climb steep hills impossible on a single geared bike.

Perhaps I should change down from my highest gear.

Most bikes, today, have what are called derailleur gears. They're so-named because the gear changer derails your bike chain from one gear cog, called a sprocket, to another.

Know your gears

Before we go further, here's a brief gear identity parade.
The heavier mechanical stuff comes in the maintenance
chapters, later on.

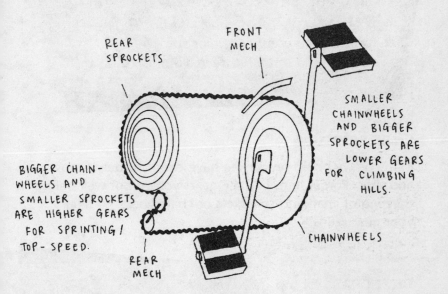

REAR
SPROCKETS

FRONT
MECH

SMALLER
CHAINWHEELS
AND BIGGER
SPROCKETS ARE
LOWER GEARS
FOR CLIMBING
HILLS.

BIGGER CHAIN-
WHEELS AND
SMALLER SPROCKETS
ARE HIGHER GEARS
FOR SPRINTING/
TOP-SPEED.

CHAINWHEELS

REAR
MECH

Cadence

The number of turns your pedals make in a minute is called
your pedalling rate or *cadence*. Keeping a regular cadence
is the secret of performance cycling. This doesn't just apply
to top racers and long distance riders, but to you as well.

An even, steady cadence (ideally 70-90 turns a minute)
uses up less energy, so you can cycle further and faster.
Constantly speeding up and slowing down your pedalling
rate wears you out more. You can change your speed, but
keep a similar cadence by using your gears. Hey, that's
what they're there for.

Gears 2

'How many gears does my bike have?'

Simple. Multiply the number of front chainwheels by the number of rear sprockets. Answers tend to be between 10 and 24.

Gear selection

Many heavy books on cycling have charts of gear ratios and stuff. Forget 'em. Use the gears you've got well before thinking of changing sprockets or chainwheels to alter your gear ratios.

HIGH GEARS for top speed on level ground.

MEDIUM GEARS for gentle up and down cycling.

LOW GEARS for lower speeds, overcoming obstacles and for climbing. Low gears give you the most control. You use them when starting off.

Gear changing

The changers on your derailleur gears need the chain running at a reasonable speed through them to do a good, smooth job. That's why you start in a low gear. It's also why you must keep on pedalling as you change gear.

Always change up or down gradually. Never change up or down a stack of gears in one go. The jolt to your legs may be a surprise, but it's a worse one for your gear mechanism and you may see your chain fly off.

Try to anticipate your gear needs.
Change down BEFORE
you need to.

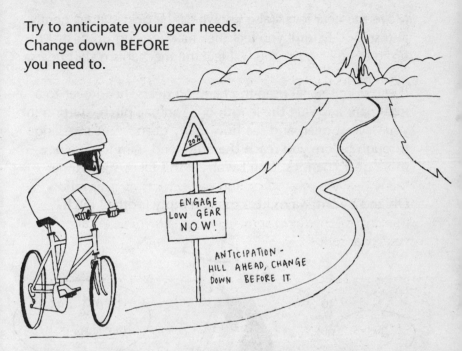

ENGAGE
LOW GEAR
NOW!

ANTICIPATION –
HILL AHEAD, CHANGE
DOWN BEFORE IT.

Finally, there's something called cross-chaining. It's easier to show as a picture.

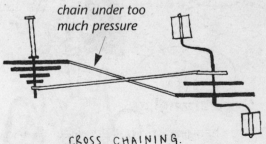

chain under too much pressure

CROSS CHAINING.

Now you've seen it, a few words of advice. Don't let it happen. The angle of the chain across the gears is too steep and there's every chance that the chain could fall off and your gear sprockets will wear out.

35

Gears 3

Hands on

Move the gear lever (also known as the gear shifter) gently and smoothly until you feel the chain moving up or down on to another gear. You will feel the mechanism shift gears.

If you're not really used to changing gears, head over to a local park and ride the length of a football pitch, starting in your lowest gear, and see how many gears you can change through before you reach the other end. Aim for five or more gear changes. Don't worry if this takes some time.

Oh and by the way, check it's an empty football pitch.

Under pressure

Putting too much pressure on your gears as you change makes it hard for the changers to work properly. This can result in a 'chain off' situation, often followed soon after by a 'rider off' situation. Modern derailleur gears can tolerate a lot of abuse, but too much pressure makes them wear out quickly and isn't a good idea.

Sometimes, though, it's hard to avoid changing under pressure. For example, when you're climbing a hill and need to change down.

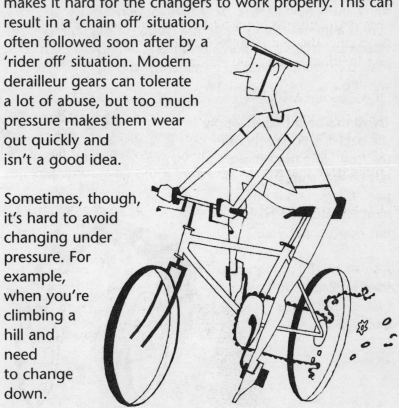

The secret is to put in a little more effort just before you change gears. Pedal faster to get your speed up and then ease off as you change gear. This gives you the speed you need to change gears successfully without the pressure on the gear changing mechanisms.

Brakes and braking

You'd be mad to start moving on something that you don't know how to stop. So know your brakes. Experience counts a lot in braking. Note how long it takes you to stop with different amounts of braking and in different road conditions. Come an emergency, you won't have time to calculate.

Try to use both brakes. Apply the back fractionally before the front. The front brake has greater stopping power. Jamming it on hard will stop the bike, but possibly not you.

Also be careful at higher speeds. Slamming both brakes on hard can lead into a skid.

STOPPING DISTANCES
AT 15 MPH.

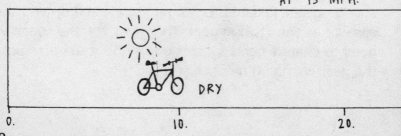

DRY

0. 10. 20.

Slowing down

Slowing down is quite different to stopping. It requires a lot less brake pressure. Concentrate on using your back brake a little more. Combine your gentle braking with changing down the gears.

Controlled braking

Such a simple thing. So effective. Controlled braking really comes into its own on steep downhill slopes or when you're cycling fast and have to stop.

Put the brakes on firmly. As you start to slow, release the brakes and start to pump them on and off. This on–off action stops them locking on to the wheel.

Keeping your brakes dry

It's one way to keep your brakes dry. Another, more practical way, is to apply your brakes lightly and often. This wipes the water off both the wheel rims and the brake shoes. Allow a lot more time for braking in the wet. Your bike can need two or three times the distance to stop on a wet road compared to a dry one.

Close control course

You can put all of the games and tests in this chapter together with some more disciplines to create a challenging course that will really help sharpen your close control skills. Remember, it's good close control skills that equal great, satisfying cycling, far more than the type of bike you have.

Set out your course on a traffic-free area of smooth, level ground. Have other riders acting as 'officials' and timekeepers. Add five seconds to the rider's overall time for each mistake. Here's one idea for a course. You don't have to stop here. Make up your own.

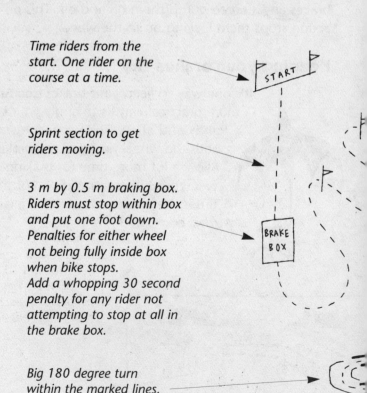

Time riders from the start. One rider on the course at a time.

Sprint section to get riders moving.

3 m by 0.5 m braking box. Riders must stop within box and put one foot down. Penalties for either wheel not being fully inside box when bike stops. Add a whopping 30 second penalty for any rider not attempting to stop at all in the brake box.

Big 180 degree turn within the marked lines.

Marker and slalom poles

Get some large, empty plastic
bottles, the ones holding squash
or fizzy drinks are fine. Half fill
them with sand or dirt. Place a
straight, thin stick or bamboo
cane into the bottle pushing
it firmly into the sand or dirt.
Tape a coloured paper flag
to the top of the marker.
This makes it easier to see.

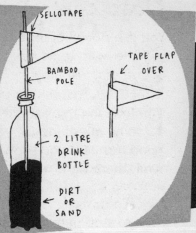

SELLOTAPE

BAMBOO
POLE

TAPE FLAP
OVER

2 LITRE
DRINK
BOTTLE

DIRT
OR
SAND

Slalom Section immediately after
braking box. Use marker poles
(see above) or large stones.
If you use stones, have someone
checking the rider's progress.

Another sprint section.

SLALOM

SPRINT

FINISH

2ND
BRAKE
BOX

TRAMLINES

'Tramline' cycling for good
balance and control. Mark
out two lines 10 m long and
15 cm wide. Five second
penalties for each time a wheel
or foot touches either line.

41

4 On the road

Safety

Before you think about skipping these pages, ask yourself some questions. Do you know how to make a right hand turn? Do you know your hand signals? Do you know what these signs mean?

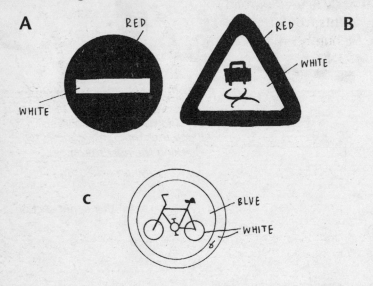

A RED WHITE

B RED WHITE

C BLUE WHITE

A = No entry.   B = Slippery road ahead.   C = Cycles only.

You should know these and all the other signs and rules in the Highway Code. All road users have to. It's the law. Yes, laws can seem silly at times, but road traffic ones aren't. They're there for the benefit and safety of everyone on the road, especially cyclists. For even with a helmet and reflective gear, cyclists are the most vulnerable of road users. The Highway Code is essential reading. It's cheap and available from any bookshop or newsagent.

Really stupid stuff

If you like cycling at all, you're not going to do the things below. Why not? Because cycling with a plaster cast is pretty much impossible. And if you do the things below, you *will* have an accident. 4000 cyclists a year are seriously injured in road accidents. You don't want to be number 4001 so **DON'T**:

Don't ride without a helmet.

Don't hang on to other cyclists or other moving traffic.

Don't carry a passenger.

Don't wear a personal stereo. You need your ears as well as your eyes on the road.

Don't ride no-handed.

Don't perform stunts on the road.

Don't swerve in and out of traffic.

Don't ride in the gutter where you can't be seen.

Safety 2

Really cool stuff

Safety isn't all, 'Don't do this, don't do that.' There's plenty of positive action you can take to make your journey safer.

- Do signal all your stops and turns.

- Do carefully check the road is clear before turning on to a major road.

- Do ride single file if with other cyclists.

- Do keep both hands on your handlebars as much as you can. If you have to react quickly, you can turn better, and stopping sharply needs both brakes applied at once.

- Do be especially careful at crossroads and junctions. Watch out for cars nudging out of side roads.

- Do leave at least three bike lengths between you and the next vehicle ahead.

- Do keep out of the gutter.

WATCH OUT WHEN APPROACHING PARKED CARS, THE DRIVER OR BACK PASSENGER MAY OPEN THE DOOR WITHOUT THINKING.

Do get off your bike if you come to a busy junction or roundabout that you're not sure how to cross. You have a huge advantage over any other road vehicle and that is you can become a pedestrian and escape a tricky traffic situation on foot.

WALK SLOWLY AT A STEADY PACE

Road riding

Road riding can be dangerous however experienced a cyclist you are. Always look round when you're first setting off and when you want to pull out or change lanes while you're cycling. Make sure the road is clear behind you. Next, signal clearly and finally, pull out and round the obstacle. Never dart out at the last minute or swerve in and out of obstructions such as parked cars. It's one of the most common causes of accidents.

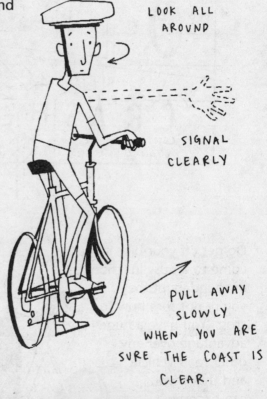

LOOK ALL AROUND

SIGNAL CLEARLY

PULL AWAY SLOWLY WHEN YOU ARE SURE THE COAST IS CLEAR.

Ride high

Make life easier for yourself by keeping a good distance away from the kerb, ideally a metre. Why? To avoid road drains, potholes and on smaller roads, excessive camber. What on earth is camber? Camber is the way a road slopes down at its edges. It's to help drainage, but on smaller roads it's a pain for cyclists. What's more, riding just a little bit further from the edge of the road makes you a lot more visible to motorists.

Making a right hand turn

The Highway Code covers all moves on the road, but let's just look at one common manoeuvre, the right hand turn.

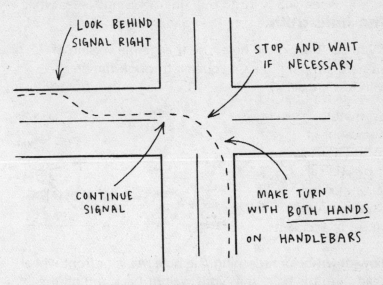

Look for a break in the traffic well before you get to the road you want to turn into. Signal and move to the right hand side of the lane. If there's nothing coming, make a right-angled turn into your road. If there's oncoming traffic, wait opposite the middle of the road you want to turn into. Hold it...and wait until there's a suitable break in the traffic.

Again, remember that if the junction looks too crowded, it's often quicker to stop, dismount and cross the road as a pedestrian.

Check out cycling proficiency courses. Your school will have details and may even run the courses at weekends or in the evenings.

Rough roads

Some roads are more like off-road trails with their bumps and potholes. These rattle you and your bike.

The hole truth

If you can't avoid the hole, use this gentle version of off-road jumping to ease yourself through the hole with less impact.

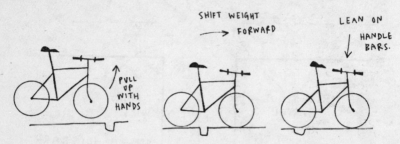

SHIFT WEIGHT → FORWARD

LEAN ON HANDLE BARS.

PULL UP WITH HANDS

Slow down before reaching the hole. As your front wheel heads into the hole, shift your weight back and off the saddle a little. Pull up on your handlebars.

As your rear wheel enters the pothole, shift your weight forward over the front wheel. Try to pull up on the rear wheel. This helps lift the rear wheel out of the pothole smoothly.

Keep your body as relaxed as possible. This helps absorb much of the bump.

Stop bumping your butt

Saddle sore and aching just from cycling around town? One way round it is to splash out a fortune on a mountain bike with full suspension. A much cheaper solution is to ease your weight just off the saddle and on to the pedals.

KEEP BOTH
LEGS BENT TO
HELP ABSORB
BUMPS.

This stops the bike bashing into your butt. Keep your arms bent to absorb some of the shock of the bumps. Experiment with using a higher gear than usual so you have to pedal less turns for the same speed.

Avoiding fumes check-list

1: Breathe through your nose. It's lined with hairs and mucus to trap pollution.

2: Use a face mask with a carbon filter. They don't stop all pollution, but they do help.

3. When you have to stop in a traffic queue, leave a bit of space between you and the vehicle in front for fresh air if you can.

4: Best of all, avoid riding in heavy traffic. Plan alternative times and routes, even if longer.

Ouch! Cycling injuries

Falling off

So you think falling off will never happen to you? Don't be so sure. Wearing your helmet and riding safely reduces the chances of serious injury. There are also a few useful falling techniques. You can't really practise these, so do read carefully.

Safe landing

As you fall, avoid landing on your bike. Cranks and handlebars suddenly become weapons. Usually, your speed of fall takes you away from your bike, but if that isn't the case, try to push away from the bike in the opposite direction.

Roll, baby, roll

It can happen to anyone. Flying over the handlebars after hitting a pothole or jamming the front brake on too hard. The secret is to try and turn the fall into a sort of forward roll. Try not to extend your hands out to break your fall. Tuck your head in and curve your body so that you land on your shoulders and roll over.

After your fall check-list

1: Catch your breath before getting up.
2: Check yourself for injuries.
3: Drink some water and rest if the fall was quite heavy.
4: Only then, examine your bike for damage.
5: If your helmet took a bashing, replace it. It's no longer serviceable.
6: If the accident is serious, make sure someone calls for help immediately. **Don't move.**

If you've had a hard fall and hit your head, **GO TO HOSPITAL.** You may feel fine, but you're not the best judge of whether you have concussion or not.

DOOOH

UURGH

51

Injuries

Some common injuries and ailments and what you can do about them.

Cuts and grazes

Wash with clean water and remove any bits of dirt. Gently apply pressure with a gauze pad until the bleeding stops. Stick a plaster over the area. Make sure the plaster's pad covers all the damaged area.

Tying a sling

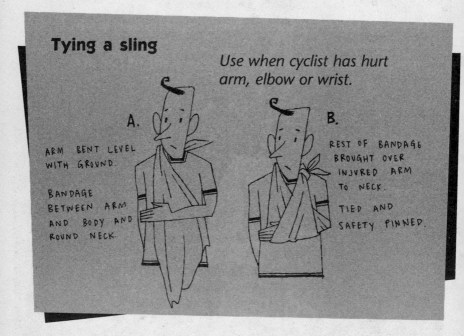

Use when cyclist has hurt arm, elbow or wrist.

A.
ARM BENT LEVEL WITH GROUND.

BANDAGE BETWEEN ARM AND BODY AND ROUND NECK.

B.
REST OF BANDAGE BROUGHT OVER INJURED ARM TO NECK.

TIED AND SAFETY PINNED.

Blisters on hands

Caused by gripping handlebars too tightly or too much weight on your wrists because handlebars are too low. Adjust handlebar height. Wear padded cycling mitts.

Sprained or pulled muscle

Loads of causes, from not warming up properly to a sudden movement. Locate the sore area and place an ice pack or a packet of frozen peas wrapped in a towel on it. Rest.

Sore knees

Probably caused by using too high a gear for too long. Rest, then continue riding in a lower gear. Also check your saddle height isn't too low (see page 16) and that your cranks aren't too long (they should be about a tenth of your height).

Headaches, cramp

Possible causes: cycling too hard; not taking in enough liquids; too much sun.
Rest in the shade. Massage the area that has cramp. Drink plenty of water.

First Aid kit

Always carry a mini First Aid kit with you. You can buy a cyclists' First Aid kit, or make your own. Pack the whole lot it a small sealable bag.

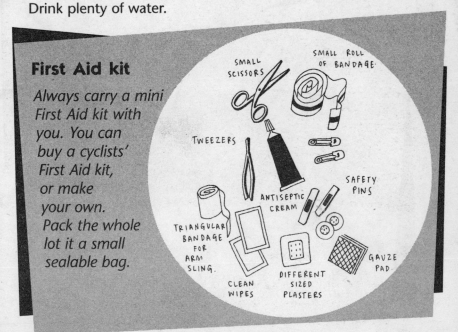

SMALL SCISSORS

SMALL ROLL OF BANDAGE

TWEEZERS

ANTISEPTIC CREAM

SAFETY PINS

TRIANGULAR BANDAGE FOR ARM SLING.

CLEAN WIPES

DIFFERENT SIZED PLASTERS

GAUZE PAD

5 Maintenance

First of all, relax. We're not going to get you to strip down your entire bike and weld bits of it. Instead, we're going to look at some simple jobs you can do which will save you a lot of cash and guarantee extra hours of cycling fun.

Your working area

I'll get help.

CHAIN TENSIONING AND REPLACEMEN

CHOOSE A FLAT OPEN AREA TO WORK IN.

CONTAINER TO PUT ANY LOOSE PARTS IN.

PLENTY OF SPARE CLEAN RAGS.

For most work, it's easiest to turn your bike upside down.

The important thing is to identify a problem and then to decide honestly whether you're up to fixing it. There's no shame in taking your bike along to a bike shop or asking a parent, neighbour or more experienced cyclist to help. Quite the opposite. Problems like the ones in the picture are best left alone.

If you want to get into fixing your bike more, there are a couple of top guides recommended in the back of this book. If not, you're best off having an annual service on your bike at a local bike shop.

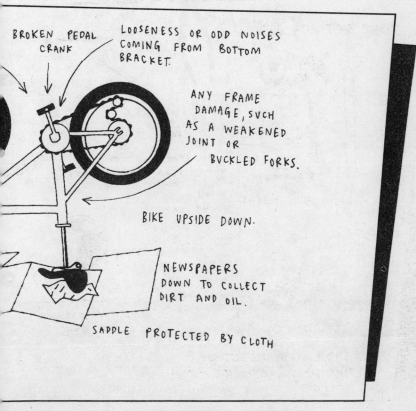

BROKEN PEDAL CRANK

LOOSENESS OR ODD NOISES COMING FROM BOTTOM BRACKET.

ANY FRAME DAMAGE, SUCH AS A WEAKENED JOINT OR BUCKLED FORKS.

BIKE UPSIDE DOWN.

NEWSPAPERS DOWN TO COLLECT DIRT AND OIL.

SADDLE PROTECTED BY CLOTH

Tool rule

You don't need as many tools as you might think. You may even be able to coax a few of these items out of your mum and dad's toolbox. Ask first, though, eh?

Minimum kit check-list

PUNCTURE REPAIR KIT

SET OF PLASTIC TYRE LEVERS

SET OF ALLEN KEYS

CHAIN RIVET EXTRACTOR & SPARE LINKS.

SMALL ADJUSTABLE SPANNER.

NARROW NOSED STRONG PLIERS

INSULATION TAPE.

CORRECT-SIZED SPANNER FOR ADJUSTING BRAKES.

SPARE BACK BRAKE CABLE (IT CAN BE CUT SHORT TO FIT YOUR FRONT BRAKE)

SPARE INNER TUBE.

BIKE PUMP

SCREWDRIVER THAT FITS YOUR BIKE'S SCREWS.

Equipment back at base

- more screwdrivers
- small hammer
- cone spanners
- headset spanner
- a sheet of rough sandpaper
- cleaning brush
- lots of clean rags
- oil
- small flat file, fine grade

Tool roll

You can make your own tool roll with a decent sized piece of strong material and some thread.

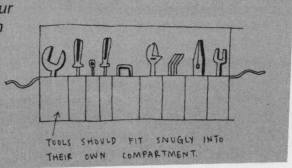

TOOLS SHOULD FIT SNUGLY INTO THEIR OWN COMPARTMENT.

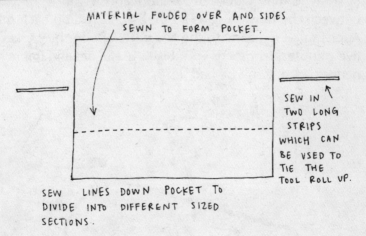

MATERIAL FOLDED OVER AND SIDES SEWN TO FORM POCKET.

SEW IN TWO LONG STRIPS WHICH CAN BE USED TO TIE THE TOOL ROLL UP.

SEW LINES DOWN POCKET TO DIVIDE INTO DIFFERENT SIZED SECTIONS.

Spares

Your spare parts box should contain at the very least: gear and brake cables, spare bulbs for your lights, valves and valve caps for your inner tubes, brake blocks, chain links and spare spokes. Oh, and lots of nuts, bolts and washers that fit your bike's parts. Broken cables can be joined with electrical connector blocks – they're easier to scrounge than new cables and most houses have some, somewhere. Build up your store of spares whenever you have some spare cash.

Lubrication: oil do that!

It's sticky, smells a bit and stains
your clothes if you're not careful.
But it's liquid magic on your bike.
What's more, it's cheap too, half
the price of a CD single.

BUY A CAN
WITH A FLEXIBLE
NOZZLE TO GET
INTO TIGHT
PLACES.

Your bike is full of moving parts. When
they rub together they heat up, can slow
each other down and cause wear. All of
these hurt performance. Bike oil in liquid
or spray form is a lubricant. A lubricant sits
between the moving parts so they don't rub on each other.
Applying oil regularly to the key parts of your bike takes
five minutes, lengthens your bike's useful life and improves
performance. Can't be bad, eh?

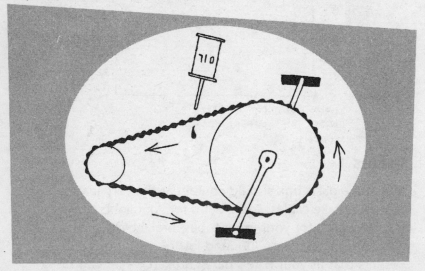

Your bike chain ideally requires a different form of lubricant.
Get a chain lubricant from any bike shop. Gently turn the
pedal as you spray the chain evenly.

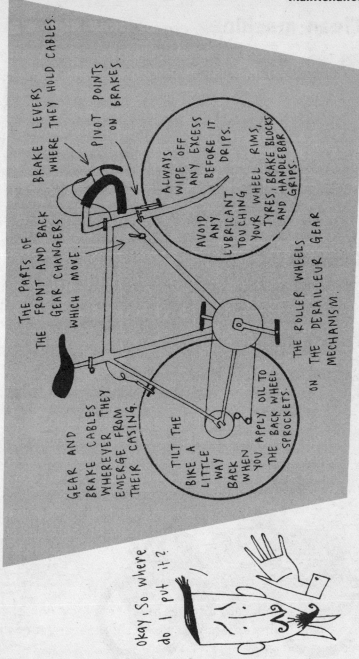

PIVOT POINTS ON BRAKES.

BRAKE LEVERS WHERE THEY HOLD CABLES.

THE PARTS OF THE FRONT AND BACK GEAR CHANGERS WHICH MOVE.

ALWAYS WIPE OFF ANY EXCESS BEFORE IT DRIPS.

AVOID ANY LUBRICANT TOUCHING YOUR WHEEL RIMS, TYRES, BRAKE BLOCKS AND HANDLEBAR GRIPS.

THE ROLLER WHEELS ON THE DERAILLEUR GEAR MECHANISM.

GEAR AND BRAKE CABLES WHEREVER THEY EMERGE FROM THEIR CASING.

TILT THE BIKE A LITTLE WAY BACK WHEN YOU APPLY OIL TO THE BACK WHEEL SPROCKETS.

OKAY, SO WHERE DO I PUT IT?

Clean machine

Cleaning kit check-list

1: Old washing-up bowl. Make sure it is an old one.
2: Old toothbrushes. Make sure they're old, too.
3: Stiff cleaning brush
4: White spirit
5: Lots of clean cloths
6: Washing-up liquid

Quick fix

Give your bike a quick clean after any long ride. It's easier to remove wet mud than dried, caked-on gunge, so wash your bike before you wash yourself. Wipe the bike dry with a cloth and lubricate the chain and other moving parts.

hmmm. Maybe needs a clean.

The full monty

Now and then, a bigger cleaning job is called for. Start by hosing or washing off all the dirt with water mixed with a tiny amount of washing-up liquid. Use a sponge for the frame and a cloth for those hard to reach places.

Wipe chainwheels with a clean piece of rag. Use the stiff brush to clean the rear sprockets.

Clean spokes, wheel hubs and rims with a toothbrush. When the bike is dry and back together, polish the frame and finally, lubricate all the moving parts.

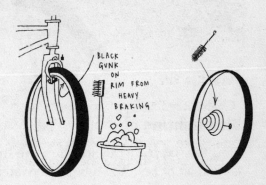

Chain gang

The chain needs a really good clean every once in a while. Unfasten the chain (see pages 72-73 for using the rivet extractor).
Place it in a basin and cover it with white spirit. Use an old toothbrush (a different one to the spoke cleaner) to scrub off the worst grime. Leave it in soak and then let it drip dry.

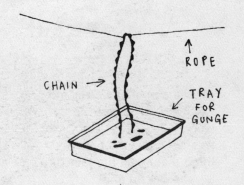

Fixing a hole

Punctures are a pain, but they only need hold you up for a few minutes.

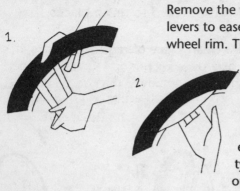

1.

2.

Remove the wheel and use tyre levers to ease part of tyre off the wheel rim. Then, hook your fingers – not the levers – under the tyre and gently, but firmly, draw your fingers around the wheel rim, easing one side of the tyre off. Pull the tube out.

Flat hunting

Find the flat by gently inflating the tube and checking for hissing air or hold the tube underwater until you spot bubbles.

CRAYON

PUMP

WATER

3.

4.

LET THE TUBE DRY FIRST.

GLUE

SAND PAPER

Mark the puncture area, and put the tube against the wheel, valve to valve hole, so you can find out where the thing that made the puncture is - and get rid of it!

Deflate the tube, then roughen the puncture area with sand-paper. Apply an even, thin layer of glue. Cover an area a little larger than the patch you've chosen.

5.

6.

Wait until the glue's almost dry. Place centre of the patch over puncture, press down firmly and make sure all the edges are sealed. Dust the patch with a little chalk to get rid of any stickiness.

Now remove anything sharp, like grit or a thorn from the inside of the tyre. By careful and do this slowly. Anything really sharp could hurt.

Refitting tube and tyre

7.

8.

Hook the tyre over one edge of the wheel rim. Place the valve through the hole and tighten the locking nut. Inflate the tube a little.

Roll the tube under the tyre and push the free edge of the tyre back on to the wheel rim. Don't let the tyre trap the tube. The last part of the tyre is the hardest to fit. Use your thumbs to push it back inside the wheel rim.

If time's short or your tube has a split, use your spare inner tube. If the old tube can be fixed, remember to repair it when you get home.

Wheels

Wheels should always be securely fastened to the frame. This may sound obvious, but loads of cyclists forget to check that their wheel nuts or quick release levers are fully tightened. This can lead to some hair-raising, wheel-losing problems.

Quick release levers

To release a wheel, pull the quick release lever outwards and flip it over, so you can read OPEN on the back of the lever. If necessary, loosen the adjusting nut on the other side of the wheel enough for the wheel to drop out of the frame.

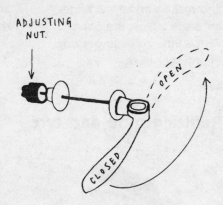

To re-fasten the wheel, start to flip the lever over to its CLOSED position, tightening the nut on the other side of the wheel to a point where the lever is sticking out sideways and is hard to move. You'll need all your strength to push it all the way over.

If it doesn't seem that tight or you're not quite sure, get an experienced cyclist to help you out.

Make sure that the lever is fully in the CLOSED position before cycling and never try to release or fasten your wheel simply by turning the lever or the nut on the other side.

Smooth running

Wheels should run smoothly. If you can wiggle your wheel from side to side, it's too loose. If you turn the wheel round by hand and it doesn't run smoothly, then it's too stiff. You'll need to adjust the wheel hubs. Get an experienced cyclist to help you.

Spokes, man

Wheels can get out of shape through bumping up kerbs and rough off-road riding. This can sometimes be sorted out by tightening or loosening the wheel spokes with a device called a spoke key. Get an experienced cyclist to help you.

SPOKE KEY

Your wheel may be just too misshapen to be saved. It's time to say goodbye and head off to the bike shop for a replacement.

Gears

Sometimes your chain just won't reach or stay on the sprocket or chainwheel you've selected. This is called under or overshifting. The good news is that both front and rear gear changers have screws which you can adjust to stop this.

Turn the high screw clockwise if the chain overshoots smallest (outside) sprocket. Turn it anti-clockwise if it won't reach it – or loosen the cable if you can't loosen the screw.

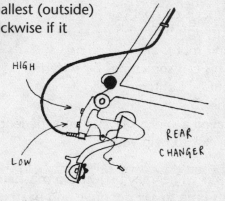

Turn low screw clockwise if chain overshoots largest (inside) sprocket. Turn anti-clockwise if chain won't reach it.

Turn low screw clockwise if chain overshoots smallest (inside) chain wheel. Turn anti-clockwise if it won't reach it (or loosen the cable).

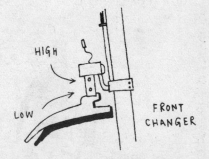

Turn high screw clockwise if chain overshoots largest (outside) chain wheel. Turn anti-clockwise if it won't reach it.

THESE SCREWS CAN BE THE OTHER WAY ROUND OR IN A DIFFERENT PLACE SO ALWAYS LOOK FOR "H" AND "L".

Front changer alignment

1 Your front changer should be parallel with your chain wheels when viewed from above.

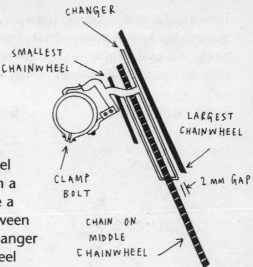

2 When the chain is set on the middle chainwheel (the inner chainwheel on a double), there should be a gap of about 2 mm between the outer plate of the changer and the largest chainwheel when viewed from the side.

Loosen the clamp bolts that hold the changer to the frame and align correctly.

Changing cable check-list

1: Put chain on smallest cog and chainwheel.
2: Loosen the anchor bolt (the bolt holding the cable in place) on the changer.
3: Pull the cable out with pliers.
4: Spray lubricant in the places that hold the cable, called housings.
5: Thread new cable in, pull it in place tightly with pliers and tighten anchor bolt.
6: Trim off any extra cable leaving 2 cm spare and fit a protective cap on it.

Brakes

They involve more fiddling than an orchestra's string section, but brakes are worth it. They come in four main types, side pull, centre pull, cantilever and top pull (V-brakes). They all run off main cables pulled by the brake lever.

Side pull brake

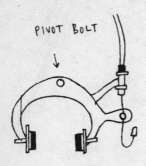

PIVOT BOLT

Centre pull brake

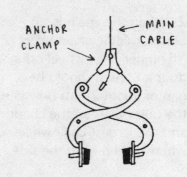

ANCHOR CLAMP

← MAIN CABLE

Cantilever brake

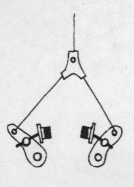

Top pull brake

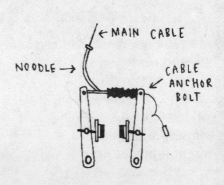

← MAIN CABLE

NOODLE →

CABLE ANCHOR BOLT

The way each type of brake makes a bike stop is the same in each case. They apply chunks of rubber called brake blocks to the rim of the wheel.

Brake blocks

The business end of brakes. All those springs and cables are designed to get the block on to the wheel rim. First of all, it's vital to keep the wheel rim and the brake block clean.

New or old brake blocks can sometimes do with a slight roughing up of their surface. Use a medium grade piece of sandpaper to give them some texture which will aid grip. Brake blocks are cheap. Replace them when worn.

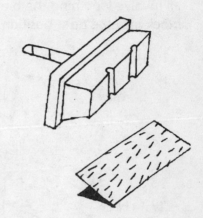

Brake cable

A worn or frayed cable is bad news.
Replace.
Undo the cable anchor bolt and use a pair of pliers to remove the cable. Fit the new cable and lubricate it.
Adjust it as above.
And fit a protective cap to stop the new one fraying, too.

Adjusting the brake blocks

As much of the brake block as possible should make contact
with the wheel rim. The following sets of adjustments should
all be done at the same time as they affect each other. They
all involve loosening the brake block nut and moving the
block into the right position.

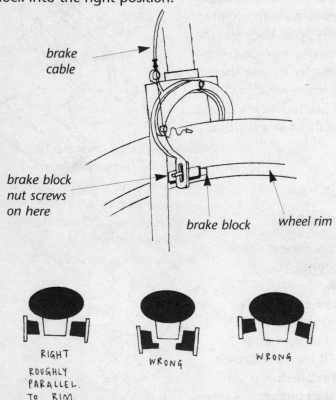

The block should be at the correct height and at the same
angle as the wheel rim. It should also be ever so slightly
angled in at the front, called toeing in. Too much toeing
in and your brakes will be weakened. Too little or none
and your brakes will squeal.

Brake mechanism

Brake blocks should rest between 1–2 mm away from the wheel rim. Further and your brakes will take too long to function. Closer and they haven't got room to move and may rub against the wheel rim even when not pulled.

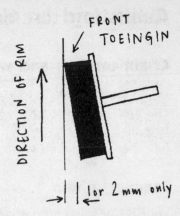

Small adjustments can be made by turning the barrel adjuster, found at the front of the brake lever or on the brake itself. Turning the barrel anti-clockwise tightens the main cable; clockwise loosens it.

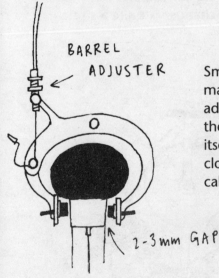

If that isn't enough, you'll need a friend to squeeze the brake blocks on to the wheel. This will allow you to undo the main cable anchor bolt or the bridge cable anchor bolt if you have cantilever brakes. Pull some cable through to tighten the brakes or let some out to loosen them. Only when you have re-tightened the anchor bolt should your friend release the brake blocks. Now check that they work as you want.

Chain and cranks

Chain tension and wear

Funny grating noises as you pedal? Lubricate chain, changers and gear sprockets. Noise still there? Get down to a bike shop and see if the chain tension is correct and whether the chain is worn.

Jammed chain

Your bike chain can get jammed. As reaching both the chainwheel and the rear gear changer is quite a stretch, get a friend to help you.

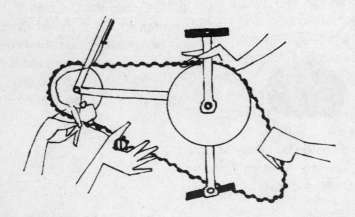

Release the tension in the chain by pushing the rear gear changer forward. Keep the changer pushed forward.

Holding the chain away from the chainwheel, turn the pedals gently backwards. Eventually, the chain will come free. Ease the rear gear changer back into position. Don't just let it spring back.

Breaking and joining a chain

When a chain breaks or gets damaged, or when you need to lengthen or shorten it, you'll need this groovy tool. It's called a chain rivet extractor. Place it over a rivet and turn the handle until the rivet has moved far enough to let you remove a link. Don't let the rivet leave the link or you'll have a tough time replacing it. You can now replace a damaged link with a new one.

Cranky cycling

Cranks can work loose with fierce pedalling. To test them, grip both cranks and try to rock them from side to side. If there is movement, called *play*, your cranks need tightening. You'll need a large Allen key (usually 8 mm) or a crank tool (usually a 14 mm socket depending on your crank's fitting).

Hold the pedal firmly as you tighten the crank by turning the tool clockwise.

If after tightening there is still a lot of play in the crank, you may need to replace the crank or have the bottom bracket overhauled. Get some help. It's a skilled job.

6 Off-road

Off-road code

When mountain biking across tracks and trails in the countryside, do use your common sense and respect others. If you can, always cycle off-road with someone else. Keep together so that if there is an accident, another cyclist can get help.

- Leave gates closed unless you found them fastened open.
- If a sign says private property, pay attention and always keep to signposted public paths.
- Never cycle next to deep water which is not fenced off.
- Always wear a helmet when off-road riding.
- Don't litter. You had room on your bike for your drinks and food, so you must have room to store the rubbish.
- Give way to walkers on paths. If the path is narrow, stop and let them pass.
- Give animals a wide berth.

Off your bike

If you reach an obstacle you cannot safely ride over, get off your bike and carry or push it past the problem.

Stand to the left of your bike (to avoid the chain and chainwheel).

Bend down with your knees. Grip the handlebar stem with your left hand. Grip the seat tube below the top tube with your right hand.

Push up from your knees, keeping your back straight. Lean the bike a little against you.

If you have to raise the bike a little higher, bend both arms up, still keeping your back straight.

Clearing obstacles

Obstacles on the trail are all part of the fun. But some fallen trees or big branches are just too big. Cycle round, or carry your bike over them. Some obstacles are small enough to jump or bunny hop over. Here's how.

Using a wheelie jump

You've heard of pulling wheelies? Well, that's how you get your front wheel to clear an obstacle like a tree root or log.

STAGE 1

Approach the obstacle head on, pedalling at a low speed. As you reach the obstacle, shift your weight to the back of the bike and pull up firmly on the handlebars. Push down on the pedals to get more lift.

STAGE 2

As your front wheel clears the obstacle, shift your weight forward to bring your front wheel down.

STAGE 3

Now, the hard part. As your front wheel hits the ground, lift out of your saddle, move your body forward over the front wheel and pedal hard. Push down on your handlebars and lower pedal. All these moves help lift the back wheel up and over the obstacle.

If your back wheel is actually on the top of the obstacle, jab down on your pedals to get the back wheel off and away.

Once away from the obstacle, move back to your normal position.

Think you're good at wheelies, huh? Check out the world record, by the Brazilian Henrique Basseto – a continuous wheelie for 10 hours, 40 minutes!

Bunny hopping

This is lifting both wheels off the ground at the same time. Sounds difficult? Well, it is reasonably hard and takes time to master, but can be useful. Looks good as well.

You'll need good toe clips (see page 108) and a low gear for this move. Stand out of the saddle and thrust your hands and feet downwards. What you're doing is compressing your bike's tyres. As the tyres respond by bouncing back into shape, leap upward, lifting the handlebars and pulling upwards on your pedals.

As you rise, prepare yourself for landing. Bend your knees and elbows to act as shock absorbers and move your weight forward.

Practice makes perfect

Practise bunny-hopping on level ground without any obstacle at all. Once you're confident of the move, practise precisely when you make the bunny hop to clear an obstacle. Cardboard boxes are great as they collapse if you mistime your hop and land on them.

I'm bushed!

On a trail, head-height obstructions can exist, too. Before you encounter a real-life bush or branch, practise ducking using your imagination.

Approach an imaginary head-high obstacle at low speed. Drop your backside behind the saddle. Crouch as low as possible, keeping your head up and looking straight ahead. Stop pedalling and freewheel under the branch or bush.

Why not make a cycle limbo bar, setting a light piece of bamboo cane (*don't* use a piece of string) that can be knocked off at heights from 160 cm to 120 cm.

HOP
NOW

Tough terrain

This is for off-road riders with a bit of experience. With all tough terrain, try to check it out first before you ride through it.

A word about riding on ice

DON'T

(I know you've seen pictures of top riders doing it, but they're top riders with years of experience and broken bones to match.)

Some words about riding on mud and sand

Always stick to your lowest gears and keep an even, reasonable speed. This is the key. Too fast and you'll lose control. Too slow and your bike will sink into the mud or sand.

Keep the front wheel up to stop it ploughing into the soft ground. Steer smoothly and gently. A sharp turn or trying to accelerate hard may force the bike to plough sideways.

Riding on angled ground

All about balance, this. Tilt the bike a little into the slope, swinging your knee nearest the slope out. To balance this movement, shift your body over to the side of the bike furthest from the slope. Keep your head as straight as possible. Keep the grip loose on the handlebar furthest away from the slope.

Rocky road

On a trail littered with rocks and stones, check to see if there is a way through. Pedal fast but ride very slowly by using your lowest possible gear. Pick a way carefully through and lift your front wheel up when you have to ride over a rock.

Riding through water

Check the depth of the water first with
a stick. If it comes up higher than your
bike's bottom bracket, you'll be doing
more swimming than cycling.

Take your feet out of the toe clips or
at least loosen the straps; you may
need to put your foot down quickly. Pick a
very low gear and pedal fast. Approach the stream at speed
and lean forward as your bike enters the water. Now transfer your weight to the back of the bike and continue pedalling hard to clear the stream. As you reach the opposite
bank, lift the front wheel slightly to clear the bank.

Concentrate on your
balance. Watch out for
the slippery, wet bottom
of the stream's bed or
you'll get a slippery,
wet bottom yourself!

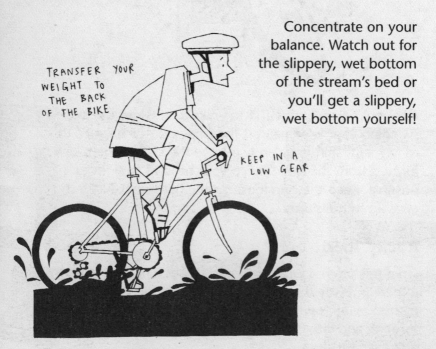

TRANSFER YOUR
WEIGHT TO
THE BACK
OF THE BIKE

KEEP IN A
LOW GEAR

Obstacle race

Seen the close control courses on pages 40-41? Why not add some elements to turn it into an off-road practice course.

Long logs, no more than 15 cm in diameter, provide excellent wheelie and bunny-hopping practice. These have to be crossed without the rider putting a foot down.

You can also simulate the close control needed when riding a rocky trail. Arrange a maze of stones and rocks which riders must pick a way through without touching a stone or putting their foot down. Make sure there is a way through, though.

Climbing uphill

Spot a bunch of map contour lines all together. They mean extra effort – a hill is ahead. Going uphill on the road calls for you to get out of the saddle. This way you can boost your pedalling power.

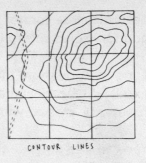

CONTOUR LINES

But a road cyclist doesn't have to worry too much about wheels gripping the ground firmly, because on a road, they usually do. On a loose or slippery off-road surface, grip is not so certain. Taking the weight off the back wheel can cause it to slip and spin, losing your hard-earned power and possibly making you skid to a halt.

CYCLIST'S WEIGHT COMES OFF THE BACK WHEEL AND MORE ON TO THE PEDALS.

The off-road answer is to stay in the saddle with your weight a little forward. This can be difficult to get used to, so first, attempt gentle uphill slopes before tackling steeper ones.

Bum on seat, but lean forward. Choose a low enough gear that allows you to still pedal very smoothly. Try to change gears before the strain gets too much. Try to avoid pulling up on the handlebars. You don't want to pull the front wheel off the ground.

Hill climbs

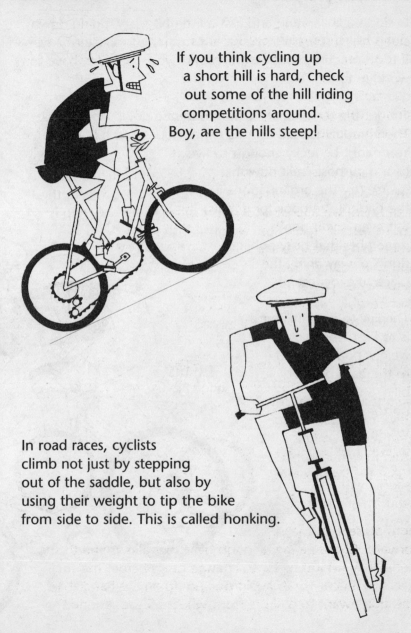

If you think cycling up
a short hill is hard, check
out some of the hill riding
competitions around.
Boy, are the hills steep!

In road races, cyclists
climb not just by stepping
out of the saddle, but also by
using their weight to tip the bike
from side to side. This is called honking.

85

Downhill riding

Exciting, exhilarating and just a little bit scary, riding down
steep hills just wasn't safe on old-fashioned roadster bikes.
It is on modern mountain bikes, but you, the rider, have to
work up to it.

Try out the techniques below on gentle down slopes first.
Then gradually build up to steeper slopes and hills.
You might be lucky enough to live
near a purpose-built downhill
course (try the organisations in
the back of the book for details).
But even if you don't,
remember that busy public
rights of way *aren't* the
place to experiment!

The key to downhilling
is to keep your body
weight both low and
to the back of your
bike. Shift your
bottom out behind
the saddle,
gripping the
back of the
saddle with
your thighs and
keeping low.

WEIGHT OVER
WHEEL

THIGHS
GRIPPING
SADDLE

Human shock absorber

Press firmly down on the pedals. Bend your knees and keep them relaxed. They act like shock absorbers easing some of the bumps of the downhill ride.

Slowly does it

Now, there are two ways to learn the next tip. You can either continue reading or you can learn the hard way by losing control on a steep downhill ride. It's up to you.

Still here? Good. You made the right decision.

PUMP BRAKING

You'll have to stretch your arms to grip the handlebars.

Riding steep downhill slopes can muddle your mind. Your speed builds up more quickly than you realise. If you don't use your brakes, within a short time you can find yourself out of control. You only know that you're out of control when it's too late to do anything about it. Keep your speed down by gently pumping the back brake. Your weight over the back wheel actually helps your back brake work better.

There's more about controlled braking on pages 38-39.

7 Touring

Touring

Cycle touring is great! Free from stuffy cars, you can really get to grips with the countryside and stop when you want to. You can go by yourself or join a group on an organised cycle tour.

Long distance trekking is serious cycling where riders pack the lightest possible gear including tents and then cycle ludicrous distances! Israeli Tal Burt completed the ultimate long distance trek cycling around the world. His 21,329 km journey took him 77 days, 14 hours.

You don't have to cycle the world to enjoy cycle touring. You'd be surprised just how much you can see in one day's riding.

Get a headstart

If you live in a town, an ideal start to your journey is
to persuade someone you know to take you out into the
country. Train services have become very picky about taking
bikes. Check beforehand that the specific line you want to
travel on will take your bike, what time restrictions there
are and if you have to make (and pay for) a reservation
in advance.

If you can't get a lift, plan a quick, safe route out of town
and into country lanes.

Bikes take up a lot of car boot space. Try these tips below.
The only remaining solution
is a bike rack,
but these are
expensive.

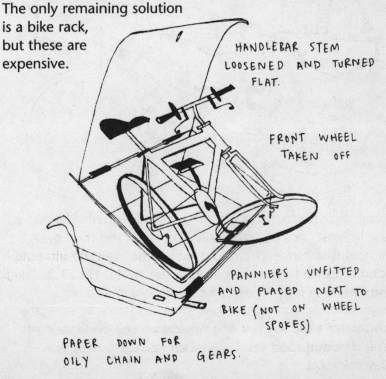

HANDLEBAR STEM
LOOSENED AND TURNED
FLAT.

FRONT WHEEL
TAKEN OFF

PANNIERS UNFITTED
AND PLACED NEXT TO
BIKE (NOT ON WHEEL
SPOKES)

PAPER DOWN FOR
OILY CHAIN AND GEARS.

Bag it!

Even a day tour requires a fair amount of stuff and a bag to put it all in. Never carry anything in a plastic bag hanging from the handlebars! You can just about make do with a small daypack with straps tight for a light day tour.

Saddlebags and panniers are much better though. They get the weight off your back and on to your bike, making cycling much more comfortable. A saddlebag is attached to the back of the saddle. Make sure it is fixed firmly. Front handlebar bags fit on to the handlebars and are ideal for valuables.

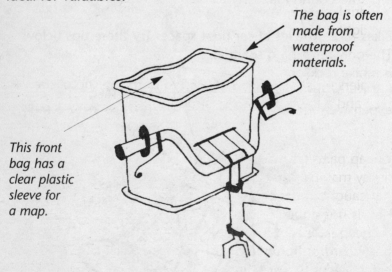

The bag is often made from waterproof materials.

This front bag has a clear plastic sleeve for a map.

For longer tours, panniers are most people's choice. They're bags that clip on to a front or rear rack. They aren't cheap but they will last a long time and let you carry lots of stuff easily.

Pannier packing

Pack your panniers equally with similar weight to keep your bike balanced. This is important. A balanced bike will be easier to ride and steer. If one pannier feels a lot heavier than the other, shift something weighty like your tool roll or a full drinks bottle into the lighter bag.

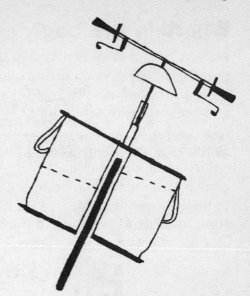

Panniers must be firmly attached to both the top of the rack and a lower point. Use strong straps.

Cheap panniers made of flimsy material can flap and get caught in the wheel. This is not good. A cheap fix is to get some hardboard or fibreboard carefully cut to just fit into the back of the pannier. This will help keep it rigid.

YOU CAN BUY HARDBOARD FROM MOST DIY SHOPS.

What's in the bag?

Map and details of your route.

Tool Roll (see page 57), pump, spare chain links, spokes, and back brake cable.

Warmer gear in case the temperature drops. A good, waterproof jacket is often essential.

First Aid kit, insect repellent and a Swiss Army styled knife.

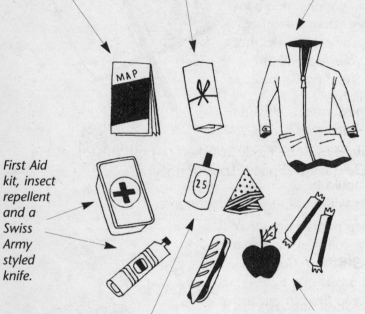

High factor sunblock for face and sun lotion for any exposed parts of body. Use a scarf or bandanna for your neck. Reapply sunblock on face as it can sweat off.

High energy, low fat foods. Fresh fruit, a decent sandwich and a couple of health food bars are fine. Take plenty of liquid with you, ideally in two water bottles, and look to stock up on your route.

Cycle computer

These little gems replaced the mileometers and speedometers of yesteryear. Get one. They're useful when trying to maintain an even speed over a long journey. Cycling computers also tell you how far you've travelled. This is valuable when touring or doing a day-long off-road ride.

Get the simplest, cheapest model possible. Unless you're racing, extra functions like lap timing and so forth are of little use. You should be too busy cycling to bother with computer programming.

Goggles

If you cycle a lot and don't wear glasses, cycle goggles are fabulous. They're usually tinted like sunglasses, but wrap around to deflect most of the dirt, grit and other unwelcome stuff that can fly up into your eyes as you cycle.

Day tour

Maps and route planning

You'll need a good map and plenty of time to study it beforehand. Build a route that buries boredom. Make sure it takes you past plenty of interesting sights along the way. A circular route is ideal as you never cover the same ground.

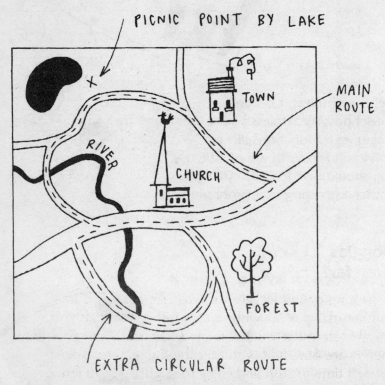

Double circle routes are a good idea for a beginner. Plan a 5–10 km smaller circle within your main circle route. Make your main circle route not too long. That way, if you finish the main route with time and energy to spare, you can do the mini-route after.

Route check-list

1: Check the route runs through villages and small towns – these will be useful stopping off points.

2: Watch out for tough hazards. For example, clumps of contour lines close together on your map may show a steep drop or climb.

3: Avoid major roads and dual carriageways if at all possible. Smaller roads are often more picturesque and interesting.

4: Find a bike shop on or near your route in advance. Jot down its telephone number.

5: Finally, leave a copy of the route with someone responsible or failing that, your parents!

How far?

There's no definitive answer. Weather, road and trail conditions, your bike and most important of all, you, will all determine what you can successfully do. First-time tourers are obsessed with mileage. Be realistic. Allow yourself time to stop and enjoy the sights. 30–50 km in a day is plenty. A little more on flat roads in good weather (not too hot and low wind) is fine. Most people can cycle at least four times as far (on road) as they can walk in the same time. (Off-road mileage counts double!)

Mileage maths

So, you've managed 20 km/h average speed for an hour-long cycle. Don't plan your route length on that speed. It's unlikely you can or would want to maintain that speed over the whole day. Use this equation instead.

Mileage   Maths

X = Number of miles mates boast of cycling

Y = Number of miles you honestly think you can do in a day

Ignore X completely

Y - 25% = Correct Mileage

Touring skills

Bring all your usual cycling skills with you, but pack a couple of new ones. One is self-awareness. Be aware of how you're feeling. If you're tired, stop. If you're feeling hot or a little dizzy, stop, rest in shade and drink plenty of water.

Check your time and distance regularly. Aim to be ahead of schedule at the half time point. You will find yourself tiring in the afternoon.

The second touring skill is navigation. Constantly check your route to see you're on the right trail or road. A compass can be useful, but for touring on roads, a decent map should suffice.

LISTEN TO A LOCAL WEATHER FORECAST BEFORE YOU SET OFF. YOU MAY REPACK OR ALTER YOUR ROUTE AS A RESULT.

Map wallet making

You can protect your map with a map wallet or make a simple one with two clear plastic document holders.

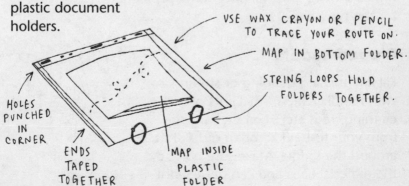

USE WAX CRAYON OR PENCIL TO TRACE YOUR ROUTE ON.

MAP IN BOTTOM FOLDER.

STRING LOOPS HOLD FOLDERS TOGETHER.

HOLES PUNCHED IN CORNER

ENDS TAPED TOGETHER

MAP INSIDE PLASTIC FOLDER

Running repairs

Some bike breakdowns can be repaired with quick fixes which might get your bike working enough to limp into the next town. Keep your cycling speed down and treat the fixed part gently. Get the problem properly repaired as soon as possible.

Slow puncture and no repair kit

Shame on you! You should always carry one. But if you haven't, take out the tube and bind the puncture area with insulation tape.

Torn tyres

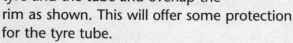

Stop punctures by packing the inside of the tyre around the rip with strong cloth, or failing that even a crisp packet sometimes works – it needs to be 10 cm long and wide enough to fit between the tyre and the tube and overlap the rim as shown. This will offer some protection for the tyre tube.

Ripped saddle

Fill any missing padding or stuffing with handkerchiefs, small bits of clothing, rags etc. Then tie bandage from your first aid kit or an old T-shirt around the saddle. Make sure none of the material flaps and can get caught in the wheel.

Big, bad, buckled wheel

If your wheel's too buckled to ride on, take it off, lean it up against a post or tree and give it a firm push with your foot. The wheel will need replacing, but you may be able to straighten it out enough to keep moving slowly for a while.

Broken cable

Tie the ends of the cable as securely as possible to a spare piece of wire, non-elastic shoe lace or toe clip strap. Use brake or gear as rarely as possible.

Broken brakes

Don't risk cycling.

Improving performance

Before you start flicking through glossy catalogues looking at new bikes and accessories, check out this chapter. There are adjustments and changes that can be made to improve performance. A few of these are to your bike, but many are to the engine that powers it - YOU!

Diet

Serious cyclists have special diets. You can read whole books about them, if you want, but not here. All we've got time for are a few common sense tips.

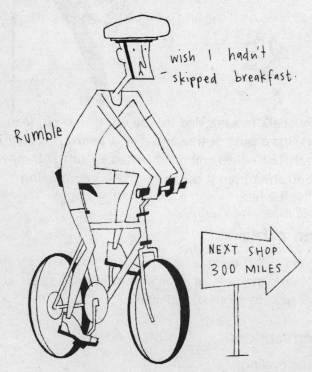

wish I hadn't skipped breakfast.

Rumble

NEXT SHOP 300 MILES

Don't go for a long cycle without having eaten that day. You may feel fine as you start off, but your energy level will drop fast.

Eat foods which contain lots of carbohydrates. These help create a substance called glycogen which produces the energy for muscles. Pasta, rice, fresh fruit and vegetables are all good sources of carbohydrate.

If you are cycling for most of the day, take some light food with you. A couple of energy or snack bars or a sandwich will make all the difference.

Don't go for a long, tough ride straight after a slap up feed. Wait for at least an hour and a half after eating a main meal before cycling hard.

Thirsty work!

A large, full water bottle is essential. Your body loses a lot of fluids as you exercise, mainly through sweat. Make sure you drink small amounts regularly. Don't just wait until you're mad with thirst and then gulp the whole bottle down.

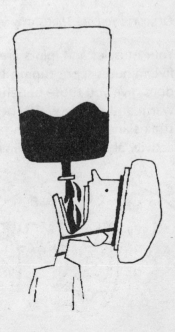

Stretching and warming up

Of course you do. That's why you should use Stretch and Go.

Your muscles and joints are precision instruments. Just five minutes spent tuning them up before cycling really does give you those benefits. Stretching gets your muscles warm and supple which helps reduce the chances of strains and pulls. Warming up gets you ready for the activity ahead with the likelihood of better performance.

Get your body warmed up by a little light jogging on the spot, a few star jumps and bunny hops and some arm swings.

WARMING UP ▶

There are many different
stretches, but here are
three common ones:

BACK STRETCH

Lie on your stomach. Place
your hands on the floor just
ahead of your shoulders. Press
up slowly keeping your hips
and stomach on the floor.

▶

THIGH STRETCH ▲

Stand upright, grip your foot
and pull it up towards your
bottom.

CALF STRETCH ▲

Bend one knee, stretch your
other leg out behind you,
sole to the floor.

Stretch check

- Make sure you're warm before you start stretching.
- Don't move sharply or bounce — ease slowly into
  the stretches.
- Hold all stretches for at least a count of ten.

Warming down

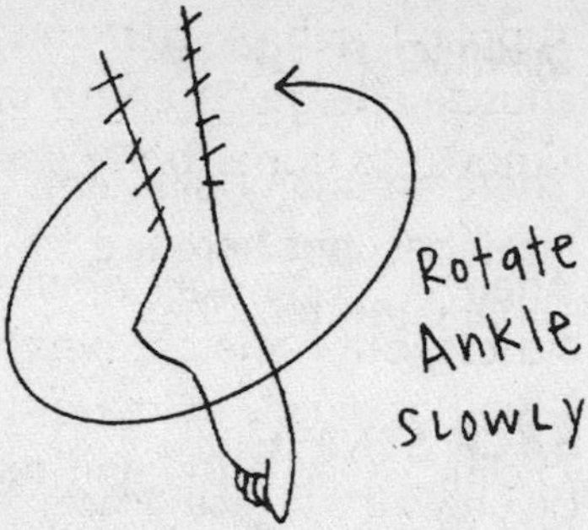

Don't stop suddenly at the end
of your cycling. Going from all
out to nothing jolts your body
badly. It can cause minor
strains and pulls.

Rotate
Ankle
Slowly

As you finish cycling, wind
down with slower and slower
pedalling. Some gentle stretching of your body including
your wrists and ankles straight after cycling helps and will
ease stiffness the next morning.

Fitness and training

Cycling uses lots of your
muscles, but in particular
four sets.

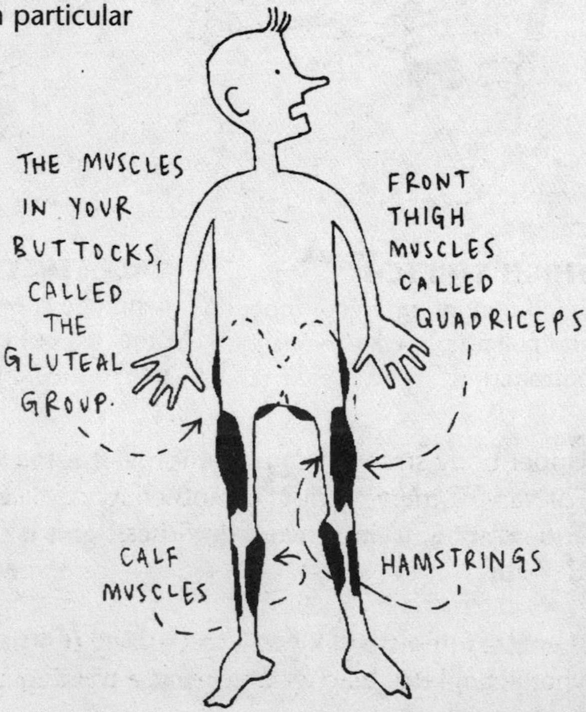

THE MUSCLES
IN YOUR
BUTTOCKS,
CALLED
THE
GLUTEAL
GROUP.

FRONT
THIGH
MUSCLES
CALLED
QUADRICEPS

CALF
MUSCLES

HAMSTRINGS

Your heart and lungs are vital. They keep your muscles supplied with oxygen and nutrients which help create muscle energy. Strength in your arms, back and neck (known as upper body strength) is also important.

There are a number of ways of improving your cycling fitness, but none are better than cycling regularly, especially if you gradually increase the distance and intensity of your cycling. Keep a training diary with details of each journey.

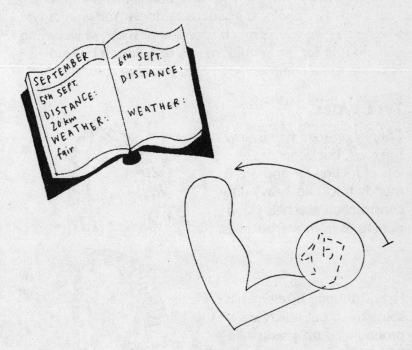

Upper body strength can be improved using weights. For variety, many cyclists use other sports, like swimming and running, to improve their fitness. This is called cross training.

If you're interested in a full-on training programme, talk to your school P.E. teacher or look at a training book or guide.

Friction

Tyres and aerodynamics

Friction is the resistance created when two objects rub together. Friction slows objects down, but it also provides grip. When a tyre rubs against the road, it grips the ground, drawing your bike forward.

Tyres are the only part of your bike that touch the ground. That's why tyre choice is a serious business. You want a tyre which can give you as much speed as possible while having enough grip for the conditions you're going to cycle in. Here are some common tyre types you may consider.

Tyre types

Chunky off-road tyre is slow on the road, but generates lots of friction for grip on muddy tracks. Its heavy duty construction also helps stop punctures from sharp stones.

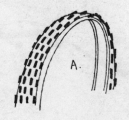

Hybrid/touring bike tyre has some tread but much less pronounced than mountain bike.

Smoother road tyre found on racers. Tread is a fine series of grooves offering maximum speed on roads.

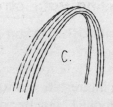

Streamlining

As you cycle, you encounter friction from the air flowing past. This slows you down. Reducing friction is known as streamlining. Streamlining becomes more important at high speeds, because the faster you cycle, the more air friction you encounter. That's why top cyclists wear skin tight clothing and specially-shaped helmets.

FLOW OF AIR

Improving your streamlining

- A good, tucked riding position helps let the air flow over you creating less friction.
- When it's safe to do so, tuck in your elbows.
- Avoid handlebar mounted drinks bottles, front bags or shopping baskets.

Boost that pedal power

Pedalling with the ball of your foot provides the most power. Sometimes, your foot can slip. Decent cycling shoes fitted with special cleats which clip on to your pedals prevent this. These allow the rider to pull back while his foot stays firmly on the pedal. Cycling up steep hills really benefits from the use of cleats. With your foot fixed to the pedal, cleats also allow you to pull the pedal round the bottom of its turn and up, creating a little more power.

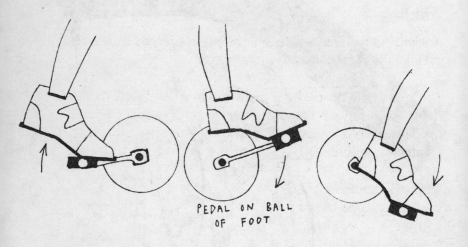

PEDAL ON BALL
OF FOOT

Toe clips

Toe clips are a holster for your foot to slip into. They also help keep your foot in place. Allow time to get used to them, especially when putting them on and taking them off.

Top clip tip

Place toe on side edge
of the pedal. Flick
pedal up.

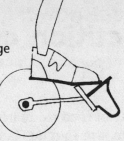

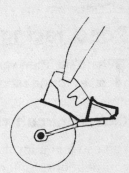

With pedal horizontal,
quickly slip your foot into
the toe clip. Keep your
toes pointing down.

Ankling

Ankling is an advanced technique using toeclips or cleated
cycling shoes to generate more power.

You've already pushed the pedal down to and past its dead
point. Now pull up firmly on your toe clip to pull the pedal
up. This coupled with the pushing down of the other pedal
creates more force.

To practise ankling, find a
safe empty area of grass
and select a very low
starting gear. Place
one foot in its toe clip.
Pedal only with this foot.
Pushing down is fine, just
like normal. But once past the
dead point, note how you have
to work hard to pull the pedal up
and round.

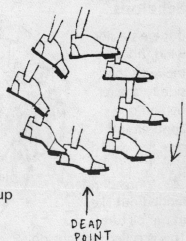

DEAD
POINT

Competition cycling

Road racing

There's a huge variety of road races, from short 40 km races to the ultimate, the Tour de France.

Closed circuit races

You can join a local club and take part in junior competitions. Junior races aren't allowed on open roads, but can take place on roads closed off from traffic. These are called closed circuit races.

Criteriums are one type of closed circuit race popular with spectators. They're high speed races over many short laps of a course usually set in a town.

Echelons

If there's a side wind, riders move to the side to shelter behind one another. If the race is a closed circuit, you will see strings of riders fanned out like in the picture. This is called an echelon.

Tactics, tactics

Road racing isn't just about flying off as fast as possible. You have to balance conserving your energy with choosing the right time to attack.

The main group of racers is known as the peloton. Often a small group of leading riders will break away from the peloton.

Time trials

Time trials are races against the clock, sometimes on roads, but also on tracks. In an hour, the very best riders can cover distances of over 55 km.

SLIPSTREAMING

Keep your speed but with less effort by tucking in directly behind another rider. The front rider takes the brunt of the air flowing past. Usually riders take turns in the front of the group. This helps the whole group travel faster.

Track racing

At speeds of up to 80 km/h, track racing is the fastest
cycle sport. Track bikes have no gears or brakes. They're
incredibly light, as little as 7 kg, just over half of your
bike's weight.

Welcome to the velodrome

The tracks on which these bikes race are called velodromes.
They're oval with steeply-banked curves. The banking is
all-important. It allows racers to corner smoothly – handy,
when you don't have brakes!

Riders can also use the banking to box an opponent
at the top or use it to swoop
down to overtake.

Sprint races

Sprint races are all about
bluff, tactics and explosive
speed. In a typical 1000 m
race, competitors don't
really go for it until the
last 200 m, the only
part of the race which
is timed. The early stages
are all about gaining the
best attacking position. Riders use all
sorts of stalling tactics to get behind
another rider, balancing almost motionless,
or faking a sprint.

SWOOPING DOWN

Pursuit racing

Pursuit riding is a great spectator sport. Two riders start off on either side of the track. If one rider catches the other at any time during the race, the race is stopped. Otherwise, the rider with the fastest overall time at the end of the distance – often 5 km – wins.

Team pursuit

Lots of fun to watch, these are pursuit races involving four riders working as a team. There's lots of manoeuvring as riders take turns at the front, with team-mates tucking in close behind.

Competition mountain biking

Good fun to watch and, when you're experienced enough, take part in, mountain bike competitions come in all different shapes and sizes.

Cross country races

Many mountain bike races are held on specially-designed courses. Riders do a number of laps of a course coping with deliberately prepared obstacles such as big logs and water jumps.

Strong leg work gets riders up tough hills, but many races are won or lost going downhill. Some riders gamble and go flat out downhill. Others are more cautious and use a zig-zagging move.

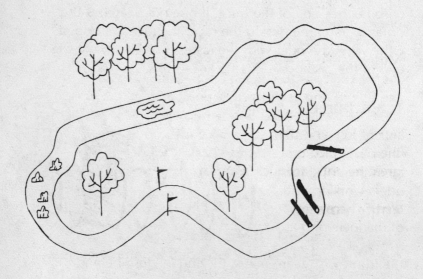

Observed trials

Some competitions aren't races
but giant obstacle courses.
The riders use all their
climbing, balancing and
jumping skills to get through
the course. Hitting a marker
or dabbing (putting a foot
on the ground) loses points.

Stunt competitions

More like skateboarding than regular cycling,
one common stunt event is the high jump.

Most riders use the table-top technique
for the high jump. The table top takes
the bunny hop as its starting point and
then goes wild! Riders bunny hop with
huge force and then turn and twist
the bike up to one side, to clear
great heights, as much as 1.2 m.

Enter yourself

Many mountain bike meets hold novice
races and trials. Contact a local club for more details
(see end of book). If you do decide to take part, try to
ride the course beforehand to get used to its hazards.

Cyclo-cross and triathlon

If you like mud and hard work, you'll love cyclo-cross. It's off-road racing, usually laps of a course, but also involves running and carrying the bike over rough ground, obstacles and up and down very steep hills.

Triathlons – the triple test

Cycling flat out too easy for you? Then why not add swimming and running as well. That's precisely what triathlon competitions do.

Course lengths vary, but at International Standard, competitors swim 1,500 m, cycle 40 km and finish off with a 10 km run. Even then, top triathletes manage an average speed of over 35 km/h for the entire 40 km cycle ride.

Triathlete cycling

Mini and junior triathlons are popular. Contact the British Triathlon Association at the back of the book for further details.

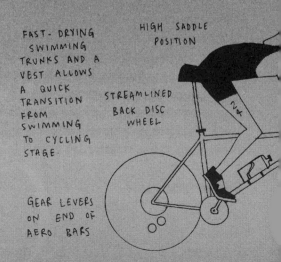

FAST- DRYING SWIMMING TRUNKS AND A VEST ALLOWS A QUICK TRANSITION FROM SWIMMING TO CYCLING STAGE

HIGH SADDLE POSITION

STREAMLINED BACK DISC WHEEL

GEAR LEVERS ON END OF AERO BARS

Cyclo-cross carrying

Good carrying technique is vital for cyclo-cross.

Grab the down
tube with your
right hand and lift
the bike so that the
top tube rests on your
right shoulder.

Loop your right
arm under the
down tube and
grip the bottom
part of the left
handlebar.

COMPETITION NUMBER,
VITAL WHEN PASSING
THROUGH CHECKPOINTS.

CHECK OUT THE
UNUSUAL HANDLEBAR
EXTENSIONS. THESE
ARE CALLED AERO
BARS AND ALLOW
THE TRIATHLETE TO
TUCK INTO A STREAMLINED
RACING POSITION.
THEY ARE PADDED
SO THAT THE
RIDER CAN REST
HIS ARMS
TIRED FROM THE
LONG SWIM.

*The very first Triathlon
was run to settle an
argument over which
sport – swimming, running
or cycling – produced the
best all-round athlete.
Still run, 20 years on, the
gruelling Hawaii Ironman
includes an enormous 180
km cycle ride sandwiched
between a 3.9 km swim
and a full length marathon
(42 km) at the end. Phew!*

Other cycle sports

BMX biking

BMX bikes are small, single geared bikes used both for racing and stunt cycling. Although they aren't much fun to cycle long distances on roads, they are great for races over short, bumpy courses with tight corners.

BMX trick or stunt cycling is fantastic to watch – even more exciting than skateboarding! The top riders fit their bikes with extra foot attachments called pegs so they can stand on all different parts of the bike and pull tricks.

Top 400 m runner, Iwan Thomas, used to be a champion BMX biker from the age of nine. He can probably run 400 m faster than he could cycle it on a BMX bike with its one gear!

Here's a complete 360° turn in the air.

Cycle speedway

Like the motorbike version, this involves
riders racing around a dirt track with tight
corners. Speedway bikes have no brakes
or gears.

To slow down round the tight
corners, riders lean heavily and
stick out their feet to slide and
pull the bike round.

Vintage bike races and rallies

The cycling version of the London to Brighton vintage car
rally, historic bike races are held all over the country in the
summer.

Bicycle polo

Polo on horses is the sport of kings. Polo on bicycles sounds
like the sport of nutters. It certainly involves a fair amount
of clattering bikes and falling off. Best left to mad adults.

The Tour de France

Make no mistake. This is THE bike race. It's the third most watched sporting event on TV (behind the Olympics and Football World Cup) and the one with the most real, live spectators. Over 13 million people line its course every year.

It's a huge test of fitness, ability and endurance. Only the very best cyclists need apply – and many of these don't finish. Over a period of 22 days, riders race a total distance of between 3,200 and 4,100 km. The race is divided into 20 or so stages starting with a sprint called a prologue and including fierce mountain climbs before ending in Paris.

Few cyclists can manage a speed of 40 km/h for more than a few seconds or minutes. Five times Tour winner, Spaniard Miguel Indurain, almost maintained that speed for the whole tour. Honest! At 39.5 km/h for over 3,900 km, the 1992 Tour was incredibly fast.

Jerseys

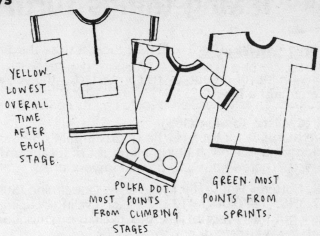

YELLOW. LOWEST OVERALL TIME AFTER EACH STAGE.

POLKA DOT. MOST POINTS FROM CLIMBING STAGES

GREEN. MOST POINTS FROM SPRINTS.

There are three coveted winners' jerseys. The yellow jersey is held by whoever is winning the race.

The green jersey is for the points winner – it is usually won by the best sprinter.

The white jersey with red polka dots is awarded to the King of the Mountains – the best climber.

Only one cyclist has ever won all three jerseys in one race and that was the great Belgium rider Eddie Mercyx. Along with Miguel Indurain, Mercyx is considered the best.

Wot no water!

Before 1972, riders weren't allowed to take on water whilst cycling. As soon as they crossed the finishing line, riders used to gulp down as much as 8 litres of water!

Taking things further

Useful addresses

There are lots of organisations connected with cycling. Here are just a few.

CTC (Cyclists' Touring Club)
More than just for tourers, the CTC is Britain's biggest cycling organisation. It holds a long list of local clubs and contacts. There's bound to be one in your area.

CTC, Cotterell House, 69 Mead Row, Godalming, Surrey GU7 3HS. Tel. 01483 417217 email: cycling@ctc.org.uk Check out their website for other cycling organisations. It's at: www.ctc.org.uk

British Cycling Federation
Lots here to do with racing and mountain biking. They also run a cycle insurance scheme.

BCF National Centre, 1 Stuart Street, Manchester M11 4DQ Tel: 0161 2302301

British Triathlon Association
Box 26, Ashby-de-la-Zouch, Leics. LE65 2ZR

British Cyclo-Cross Association
14 Deneside Road, Darlington, County Durham DL3 9HZ

For reflective clothing, patches and strips, try **Technicolour Tyre Co.** PO BOX 373, Brookwood, Woking, Surrey GU24 0BA

Raleigh is one of the biggest and best manufacturers of bikes and accessories. They can be contacted at Triumph Road, Nottingham NG7 2DD

Australian Cycling Federation Inc.
14 Telopea Ave
Homebush NSW 214
Tel: (02) 9764 2555

Bicycle NSW
GPO Box 272
Sydney NSW 2001
Tel: (02) 9283 5200

NSW Cycling
P.O. Box 895
Bankstown NSW 2200
Tel: (02) 9796 1344

Bicycle Federation of Australia
email: icycle@ozemail.com.au

Also try this great Australian biking website at:
www.jub.com.au/cycling/

Books

Richard's New Bicycle Book
Richard Ballantine
Oxford Illustrated Press

The Bicycle Touring Manual
Rob Van Der Plas
Bicycle Books

All Terrain Biking
Jim Zarka
Bicycle Books

Cycling Plus Fitness for Cycling
Richard Howat

Cyclists' Training Diary
Spiral Books

Maintenance Guides

The Bicycle Repair Book
Rob Van Der Plas
Bicycle Books

The Bike Book
Haynes Manuals

Magazines

Plenty of cycling magazines around at the moment, but all tend to be for the serious adult cyclist with money to burn. Of the bunch, *Total Bike* is the best. It's fast reading, witty and cool. Most of all, it offers honest and thoroughly tested reviews of equipment.

Maps

Scale is important. Look for 1:50,000 for touring and straightforward trail riding and 1:25,000 for serious off-road riding. Ordnance Survey (O.S.) maps are excellent. Other good maps are available from the CTC (see page 122).

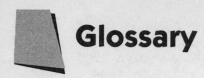

Glossary

Allen key Six-sided tool used to adjust Allen bolts often found on your brakes and gears.

Alloy Usually a mixture of metals that make a lighter, stronger bike part.

Axle The rod which the wheel hubs rotate around. Also found in the bottom bracket.

Bars Handlebars

Block The collection of gear sprockets on your back wheel.

Bottom Bracket The joint between the down and seat tubes, inside which is the axle that joins the two pedal cranks.

Clearance The distance between the bottom bracket and the ground.

Crank The arm that joins a pedal to the bottom bracket.

Dust cap Protective covering often covering crank fitting.

Freewheel Cycling without pedalling. Used to cruise down hills.

Knobblies Heavy tread tyres found on mountain bikes.

Mitts Short for track mitts — the fingerless gloves used by many cyclists.

psi Pounds per square inch — still the most common measure of tyre pressure.

Rear Triangle The back end of the bike.

Slicks Racing tyres with no tread.

Truing Straightening a buckled wheel.

Tubular tyre (or tub) Tubeless tyre used on racing bikes, often cemented to the wheel rim.

Wheelbase The distance between the axles of the back and front wheel.

Index

ACTIVATORS

All you need to know

0 340 715162	Astronomy	£3.99	☐
0 340 715197	Ballet	£3.99	☐
0 340 715847	Birdwatching	£3.99	☐
0 340 715189	Cartooning (Sept 98)	£3.99	☐
0 340 715200	Computers Unlimited (Sept 98)	£3.99	☐
0 340 715111	Cycling	£3.99	☐
0 340 715219	Drawing (Sept 98)	£3.99	☐
0 340 715138	Football	£3.99	☐
0 340 715146	The Internet	£3.99	☐
0 340 715170	Riding	£3.99	☐
0 340 715235	Skateboarding	£3.99	☐
0 340 71512X	Swimming (Sept 98)	£3.99	☐

Turn the page to find out how to order these books

more info • more tips • more fun!

ORDER FORM

Books in the Activators series are available at your local bookshop, or can be ordered direct from the publisher. A complete list of titles is given on the previous page. Just tick the titles you would like and complete the details below. Prices and availability are subject to change without prior notice.

Please enclose a cheque or postal order made payable to Bookpoint Ltd, and send to: Hodder Children's Books, Cash Sales Dept, Bookpoint, 39 Milton Park, Abingdon, Oxon OX14 4TD. Email address: orders@bookpoint.co.uk.

If you would prefer to pay by credit card, our call centre team would be delighted to take your order by telephone. Our direct line is 01235 400414 (lines open 9.00 am – 6.00 pm, Monday to Saturday; 24-hour message answering service). Alternatively you can send a fax on 01235 400454.

Title .... First name .... Surname ....

Address ....

....

....

Daytime tel .... Postcode.............................

If you would prefer to post a credit card order, please complete the following.

Please debit my Visa/Access/Diner's Card/American Express (delete as applicable) card number:

Signature ....Expiry Date ....

If you would NOT like to receive further information on our products, please tick ☐ .